the low
road to
new
heights

the low road to new heights

What It Takes to Live Like Christ in the Here and Now

Wellington Boone

 Doubleday New York London Toronto Sydney Auckland

PUBLISHED BY DOUBLEDAY
a division of Random House, Inc.
1540 Broadway, New York, New York 10036

DOUBLEDAY and the portrayal of an anchor with a dolphin are trademarks of
Doubleday, a division of Random House, Inc.

Book design by Chris Welch

Cataloging-in-Publication Data is on file with the Library of Congress

ISBN 0-385-50087-4

PRINTED IN THE UNITED STATES OF AMERICA

July 2002
First Edition

1 3 5 7 9 10 8 6 4 2

The following versions of the Bible are used in *The Low Road to New Heights:*

*I dedicate this book to all of those who see
this road as a way of life that God can use
to bring us to new heights.*

contents

the low road to new heights

how can I become more like Christ?

"God . . . gives grace to the humble." —1 PETER 5:5

JEFF IS JUST about ready to give up on trying to live the Christian life. Everywhere he goes he keeps running into the same problem. People can be impossible to live with—forget trying to treat them as Jesus would treat them, in a way that honors God. Ever since becoming a Christian several years ago, Jeff has tried hard to be kind and patient, even with the most difficult people. But then something catches him off guard. A degrading comment. A thoughtless act. In a split second, a flash fire of anger blazes up inside of him, and he lashes out.

Yesterday, during a staff meeting at work, Jeff was trying

to explain a new plan he wanted to try, when Bill started asking questions about the idea. Instantly, Jeff's anger flared, and he said defensively, "I'm not sure you're in any position to cut me down. I haven't seen many good ideas coming from your direction lately."

Bill's face reddened with embarrassment. "I wasn't criticizing you, Jeff," he said quietly. "I think you have a great idea. I was asking questions because I really want to understand your whole plan, so I can know how to support you."

Ever since that moment, Jeff has wondered what it is going to take to make him a better Christian. Nothing he does seems to change him. That old excuse he's used for himself—"Christians aren't perfect, just forgiven"—isn't working anymore. Privately, he thinks, *If people can't see Christ in me, I might as well shut my mouth . . . and quit trying.*

Jeff thinks that Cheryl is the finest example of a Christian he knows. Cheryl never opens her mouth to cut people down. He thinks, *I've never even seen her get angry. I wish I knew her secret.* Cheryl's "secret" is that she feels like a spiritual failure, too. True, she doesn't lash out the way Jeff does. Her tendency is to harbor negative thoughts and feelings about people inside. These negative feelings turn into bad attitudes—like envy and jealousy, or judgmentalism. Actually, she *is* lashing out. She just does it in the form of quiet rejection. She knows she's not the "nice" and "loving" Christian others think she is. Once in awhile, in a church service, she will hear a convicting message that makes her feel guilty about her attitudes. But when she tries to change, nothing seems to work for her.

When Cheryl thinks of how defeated she is, she thinks about Pastor Smith. He seems like such a good man. She wishes she could be half the Christian he seems to be . . . And at this moment, sitting alone in his study, Pastor Smith wonders why he ever got into the ministry. He thinks, *Some of these people I can't even deal with. In fact, a lot of them make me want to get in the flesh and just boot them out the door.* Something inside him wants to rise up and say, *Look, this is my ministry. If you don't like it here there are plenty of other churches nearby.*

There are two deacons who always have axes to grind. About a dozen people in the congregation rub him the wrong way. And one woman in the church always seems to have some kind of high-pressure agenda. Pastor Smith hesitates to talk openly about his spiritual life with other pastors. They always appear to be so together, and he doesn't like to admit things aren't working for him. Some voice inside says, *Just act cool. Never look weak.* In calmer moments, however, he thinks, *Didn't I follow this "calling" because I wanted to help people change and grow spiritually? How can I help others change, if I'm not becoming more like Christ myself?*

All three of these people share some things in common. All of them feel as if they're in a war. On the one hand they want to grow in spiritual strength, love and maturity, but on the other hand, a very un-Christian impulse seems to win most of the time. Somewhere inside, each one wants to know, *How can I be more Christ-like?*

The Battle

Maybe you are experiencing the same battle that's going on inside Jeff, Cheryl, and Pastor Smith. Welcome to the warfare of the Christian life. Under normal circumstances, most of us can act and look and feel like decent Christians. We can quote Scriptures. We go to church. But we don't really find out what our nature is like until we are under pressure. What happens when somebody steps on us? That's when we find ourselves in a real struggle.

If most of us Christians are honest, in many ways we are like snakes. We hold unforgiveness, and we're ready to rise up and strike. When people walk on us, we find devious ways to "get even." When people criticize us, we respond with words that have a bite like poison. As Christians, we don't want to have this nature in us. But most of us don't know how to change. I know I didn't. I had to learn that the very challenges I was facing were the instruments of God to change me.

Take the criticism I receive from my wife, for example. Like most men, I didn't want her to tell me the truth about myself. I didn't recognize that God had placed her in my life, in part, to point out my weaknesses. My wife sees the real me more than anyone else. By learning to allow her to make comments without striking back, I've discovered that her words are always tools to help me to change—*if I see them as tools in God's hands.*

But that's the problem for so many of us. We say we're Christians and that we have surrendered to God. But the truth is, we're really in submission to everyone else. By that I mean we allow every comment, every attitude, every raised eyebrow to go straight to the heart, and we react. That's because we are more concerned with what people think and say about us than about God's opinion of us.

The problem is not really with other people, though. We may want to blame them for triggering our reactions, but the truth is this: By their words and actions, they step on something that lies coiled inside each one of us. That is our old nature. *Pride.* The nature of the snake that inhabits every one of us fallen creatures.

In the Garden of Eden, Satan fed the pride of the first people by suggesting that they question God. The first commandment is to love God with all your heart, soul, mind, and strength, but Satan immediately undermined that relationship in the Garden by causing the woman—and the man, who was there listening—to believe that God was not worthy of their love at the level of total obedience, and that God had not provided all that they needed to get their needs met. They came into the world as adults in the image of God, but he reduced them down to disobedience by his influence on their minds.

At any age you have the potential to regress and become a spiritual child in your relationships with God and other people. That's why you have to be constantly on the alert, watching for the devil. The Bible says, "Be sober, be vigilant; because your adversary the devil walks about like a roaring lion, seeking whom he may devour. Resist him, steadfast in the faith, knowing that the same sufferings are experienced by your brotherhood in the world. But may the God of all grace, who called us to His eternal glory by Christ Jesus, after you have suffered a while, perfect, establish, strengthen, and settle you. To Him be the glory and the dominion forever and ever" (1 Peter 5:8–11).

In our marriages, we tell ourselves it's our spouse's words and actions that are the problem. But most often it's our pride. We harbor anger. We resent being criticized and we rise up and fight back. In time we finally get fed up with those comments and decide to break covenant and get a divorce. Why? Because we are looking at that man or that woman instead of looking to God and asking Him to humble us so we can look honestly at ourselves. When we leave God out of our "looking," the Bible would say that our eyes are evil. We are looking at things outwardly—at what our mate is saying that we don't like. God wants us to look inside and see the pride in our own heart (see Mark 7:21–23). He wants us to make our spiritual development the highest priority, instead of looking at our need to be loved. In this way every word spoken to us, every action for or against us, can become a tool in the Lord's hands to minister truth and growth in Christ-likeness. Over the nearly thirty years that I have been married, I have learned from my wife many times how imperfectly I was walking out the Christian life.

The mark of a Christian is, in Paul's words, that we bring "the sweet savor," or the essence, of Jesus Christ wherever we go (see 2 Corinthians 2:14–16). Instead of stinking up the place with our fleshly attitudes, we create the sweet-smelling environment of heaven on earth with our Christ-like attitudes. When people hear us speak or watch our lifestyle, they should be able to witness the character of Christ in us because His nature is growing within us.

Stepping Down

Throughout Church history, one of the most important words that has defined the nature and character of Jesus Christ has been humility. Humility has been called the cardinal virtue of Christ by giants of the Faith from Paul to Augustine to Andrew Murray. But it is a word most of us use lightly, without really knowing what it truly means.

Humility is a heart attitude that allowed love, kindness, patience, peace, and every other spiritual quality to pour out from Him into the people He encountered every day. Humility is an attitude of spirit that describes Jesus Christ, and it's also an attitude that we need if the character and spirit of God are going to grow in us and shine out from us into this dark world. Jesus displayed humility when He set aside His glory and came to live among men, stripping Himself of all that was due to Him as God.

I want to make this plain from the outset: When Jesus came to live among us, He had to step down from a higher position. He was and is God. When He "became flesh and dwelt among us," as the apostle John puts it (John 1:14, KJV), He willingly left a higher place and stepped into a lower place (see Philippians 2:5–11). By doing that, He gave dignity to our humanity, and in that sense He gave us something of an elevated status. He confirmed that we are more than the dust we're made from—and we are not just animals somewhere on the evolutionary ladder. What we need to learn, however, and to practice, is the course of action Jesus took over and over again throughout His earthly life. He humbled Himself. Not one time only, but again and again.

Now as we've seen, when Jesus humbled Himself He had to step down from a higher place to a lower place. He came down from heaven to earth. He entered into a body that is subject to all the mess we're subject to—the temptations, the ravages of time, the weaknesses of the human body. All of it. When you are God, that's a definite step down!

Jesus' whole life was an example of surrender to the Father's will, right on up to the cross. It was on the cross that His surrender was fully exposed. He refused to strike back at His enemies. Instead, He cried out for their forgiveness. Jesus let the Father crush Him for the sins of the world. He stayed on the cross in agony until He fulfilled all that God had intended for Him and His creation.

From a great messianic psalm, which Jesus quoted on the cross, comes this confession from His inmost being:

"But I am a worm, and no man; a reproach of men, and despised by the people" (Psalm 22:6, KJV). Jesus called Himself a worm because He led a surrendered life, and died a surrendered death. When it was time to return to His Father, He could say, "It is finished" (John 19:30). He had never changed His mind about His surrender. He was the greatest example of humility the world has ever seen, and we are called to follow Him in His humility.

For us, humility is the attitude that helps us to find our place of destiny in the rank and order of things. It gives us a more accurate picture of ourselves, as God sees us. Now what does that mean?

What We Need To Know About Humility

Most of us tend to puff ourselves up. We want people to see us as bigger and better than we are. We think, *Can't they see how important I am?* We also tend to see *ourselves* as bigger and better than others. We look at other people and think, *I would never do that. I would never say a terrible thing like that.* At the same time, we believe we deserve better treatment than we're getting. We think, *No one should speak to me that way. No one should act like that toward me. They should be treating me better than that.*

When we think this way, and we spend our lives fighting

to protect the threatened and demanding little person inside of us, we aren't free. We're chained to everyone else's opinion of us. We are reacting to everything people say and do—anything that shows they are thinking less of us than we imagine ourselves to be. As Paul would say, we think more highly of ourselves than we ought to think (see Romans 12:3). We are stuck in a daily struggle to elevate ourselves in the eyes of others. Now, if we're so busy fighting to protect ourselves and our own agenda, where do we find the time or energy to go out and do what God asks us to do? When do we go out in His name to love and serve other people and bring them into His kingdom?

The first thing we need to know about humility—the Christ-like attitude that directs us to lay aside our pride and give up our rights and demands—is that humility sets us free! Humility releases something on the inside of us. It gives us the ability not only to take our rightful place in the world, but also to take a position *lower* than everyone else— like Jesus, who came down to serve all mankind, taking the lowest place of all. Only after He lowered Himself did God raise Him to His rightful place. As Paul wrote,

He humbled Himself and became obedient to the point of death, even the death of the cross. Therefore God also has highly exalted Him and given Him the name

11

which is above every name, that at the name of Jesus every knee should bow, of those in heaven, and of those on earth, and of those under the earth, and that every tongue should confess that Jesus Christ is Lord, to the glory of God the Father—PHILIPPIANS 2:8–11.

The "Practice" of Humility

Humility sets us free. But humility requires practice because it doesn't come naturally. Lashing out comes naturally, but not lowering ourselves!

Somehow we have the wrong idea about the spiritual life. We think we can just get a new idea in our heads from the Bible and—bam—we have it. But growing in the character of Christ is not like learning the times tables. We learn it—that is, it is worked into us—only as we learn to practice the utterly humble, God-dependent attitudes of Jesus in the face of every challenge and opposition that the world, the flesh, and the devil throw at us. That takes time and continual recommitment to taking the low road, with Jesus.

The practice of humility is the secret to strength and maturity in the Christian life. To learn humility is to discover the way to have God's Spirit grow strong within you. Andrew Murray, the great nineteenth-century missionary pastor to South Africa, wrote: "Just as water ever seeks and fills the lowest place, so the moment God finds the creature abased and empty His glory and power flow in to exalt and bless."[1] It was because of Murray's Christ-like humility that God was able to bring massive revivals to South Africa during his life and ministry. The kind of genuine revivals we are in need of today.

Death to Life

Everywhere I go, Christians are praying for "revival." I myself believe that a great revival is needed. Quickly. When most folks hear the word "revival," what usually comes to mind is several days of meetings with perhaps some miraculous healings and hundreds being saved. However, revive really means "to bring to life again." And what God must bring to life, if He is going to draw the world to Himself in these final days, is the sweet savor of Jesus Christ in *us*—in Christians. Christians must be revived—brought back to the life of Christ within them—before they will be able to awaken the world.

In order for the nature of Jesus Christ to come alive in us, something in us must first die—our pride. But we don't want to die. We want to strut our stuff, to prove to ourselves and the world that we are "something else"—something special. When we act like that, we are really missing it. Our hearts are deceived. As the prophet Jeremiah put it, "The heart is deceitful above all things and desperately wicked; who can know it?" (Jeremiah 17:9).

We can fool other people about the condition of our hearts, but not God. Samuel was almost fooled by the outward appearance of the brothers of David when he went to Jesse's house looking for the next king of Israel. God was able to see their hearts, and He was able to see David's heart. He knew that David was the one (see 1 Samuel 16:7). God knows our hearts, too.

If we want God to revive us so that our hearts come alive with the spirit and character of Jesus Christ, we must first come to the end of ourselves—not once, but continually. We must always be ready to admit that we need God. It's no good trying to manage our sin, or cover up our behavior so that we look like good people on the outside when we are really rotten on the inside. Instead, we have to go to the cross and die daily (see 1 Corinthians 15:31).

When it comes right down to it, most of us struggle with surrendering our lives to the jurisdiction of God, so we find ourselves rising up against God—our will crossing His will. Whenever we are in conflict with God, we need to die. We never win when we cross wills with Him. We always lose. Our fight for independence is a loss every time. Our only option is to surrender our self-will and give in to God. We need to receive the nature of Jesus and say, "[N]evertheless, not as I will, but as You will" (Matthew 26:39). When we willingly follow God's direction and take the low road, the path of humility, we have come to a new beginning. It is not an arrival, but it *is* a beginning. It is something that God can work with. It is the entrance into a process that works everything out of us that resists the will of God.

Coming into Christ-likeness is a process. It takes time to replace attitudes and opinions that have been resisting the infilling of the new life of God in Christ. That old self-will has got to be brought low so that it will die. This is a lifetime work of every Christian.

The call to lowliness and total dependence upon God is not popular in this day of the "self-made" man and woman, yet it has been proven in the life of Jesus Christ and in those who have followed Him through the centuries. When we submit to Him, He helps us. When we lower ourselves, He raises us up. When we honestly admit we're confused or doubtful, He gives light and a fresh breath of faith. When we lack knowledge, He gives understanding. As the Apostle James wrote, "Humble yourselves in the sight of the Lord, and He will lift you up" (James 4:10).

Had Enough?

At the outset, we saw the frustration of three Christians who probably spoke for many of us. They had struggled to be "better Christians" using their own self-will, as many of us have, but had not tapped into God's strength. Haven't we had enough of trying to live the Christian life in our own strength? Are we ready to surrender to the power of God? Many sports fans have heard about the famous WBA welterweight title bout in 1980 between Sugar Ray Leonard and the Panamanian fighter, Roberto Duran. It speaks to me about my own stubbornness and knowing when to given in.

Sugar Ray was already a national hero for winning an Olympic gold medal. The bout with Duran was one of his first pro fights, and the world championship was at stake. Duran fought tenaciously for seven rounds, even though he was sorely outmatched. By the eighth round, he was losing so badly that he finally cried out, *"No más! No más!"* ("No more! No more!")

We tend to keep fighting to keep our pride, but when we decide that we have had enough of our old self-life and give in to Christ's life in us, we have reached a new beginning. For some of us, sadly, it takes getting pummeled, like Duran, before our inner man bows before God. For me, the first time I really surrendered to God was the time when I turned myself over to Him and was saved. Like most people, I had to be broken before I understood what it means to let God have His way. I was going my own way, but God interrupted me and came to me with such a Shekinah* glory that there was no mistaking what He wanted from me. I had been a backslider before that, but after He broke through to me that time, I never turned back. I just wanted to yield to Him and please Him from then on.

I have not attained perfect humility, and I do not have the right heart attitudes all the time, as if the character of Christ is something that I seized once and now have forever. However, something changed inside of me, and from then on I have wanted God to perfect my heart attitudes of humility. If we practice humility over a period of time, eventually it begins to take root in us and reform our thoughts and actions.

---

* "Shekinah" means a visible, light-filled manifestation of the presence of God. Shekinah was used to describe times when God came in some visible form such as on the altar of the Holy of Holies, with Moses on Mount Sinai (Exodus 24), or when Solomon dedicated the temple (1 Kings 8). After the Babylonians destroyed it, the Shekinah glory did not return to future temples, but occasionally individuals see the light-filled presence of God in their personal experience.

From that time on, however, I can say that I have understood the life of the Christian in a whole new way—and I have experienced the continual infilling of the Holy Spirit and the life of God of which Andrew Murray spoke. Truly, I could begin to see the old passing away, and the new life of Christ dawning more brightly in me.

Born Again?

Since the 1940s, we have seen the spread of the Gospel like no other time in history. Yet most major evangelistic ministries observe that, for all the people who make public commitments to God during crusades, a relative few go on to live out the Christian life in any effective way. Jesus Christ obeyed and served His Father. Is that what being a Christian means to you?

The truth is, we all serve something. What do you serve? Is it your work? Your family? Your reputation? Maybe it's your husband or wife. For many today, it is the god of comfort. They think, *Whatever seems to make me happy, that's what I'll give my energy and time to*. To the extent that our will rises up to follow anything that is not the true God, we are not followers of Jesus Christ. To the extent self-will remains in us, the nature of Christ cannot grow in us.

In much of contemporary Christianity, we are hearing a

resurgent emphasis on personal accountability. On one hand this is a good thing, because ignoring sin or covering it up is not healthy. It's like refusing to take care of an infected cut and allowing the infection to spread. As the apostle Paul said, "The wages of sin is death" (Romans 6:23), and hiding our sin brings death to the spirit.

But too often our idea of becoming accountable to one another winds up focusing on changing our outward behavior. Jesus referred to this as cleaning the outside of the cup without cleaning the inside (Matthew 23:25). When we begin the process of examining our heart attitudes, we experience a removal of the self-will that is the root of sin. That's when we start to change from the inside out. Staying focused on our sins and trying to manage them isn't going to change us in the long run. We might look good to a few people for a while. We might even fool ourselves, but eventually, the wound needs to be cleaned. Our growth as Christians—as those transformed by Christ—must begin on the inside.

Looking Like Jesus

The world needs to see Jesus again. We ourselves—Christians—need to see Him. No one painted a picture of His face. I believe that is because He had no intention of leaving us a physical likeness. The image of Christ that God wants to hold up before the world is us. We are made in the image of God, and we will reflect that image to the degree that we surrender our innermost will to the will of the Father.

Ask yourself right now: What areas of my life are not surrendered to the will of the Father? Am I afraid to submit my health and well-being to Him? My children or my spouse? Have I offered Him a small piece of my income—but not surrendered all my earthly substance for His use? Deeper still, have I given Him the whole force of my will—my dreams, goals, aspirations?

Every area that is not submitted to God is an area where we need training in Christ-like surrender. Humility training. Only then will we know the transforming power of Jesus Christ, giving new strength and Christian maturity within.

Stuck on the Way

I offer this book to every Christian who feels stuck along the road in the Christian journey, to everyone who began the Christian life with excitement and with hope that they would find new life in God. Many of us have found ourselves sidetracked, stuck on the way—even backtracking and returning to our old desires for what this world has to give. We feel there is a gap between what we say we believe as Christians and how our hearts secretly tell us to live. We feel powerless to change, instead of becoming the living witnesses for God that we had hoped to be.

Learning the practice of humility is the beginning of total spiritual transformation. It is the attitude that gradually brings our straying and disorderly will into line with the purpose and plan that God the Father has for each one of us. We begin to learn how to pray as Jesus prayed, how to love our enemies the way Jesus loves, how to live righteously in the face of evil, how to step beyond our small selves to give our lives for God's greater purpose. And gradually, a new image forms within us—an image that becomes clearer and more brilliant every day. It is the image of Christ, risen and bright, coming out of the tomb in which our old nature has died (2 Peter 1:2–4).

A Prayer for You

What follows is not a "program" for spiritual growth and change. It is more an opportunity to learn some of the ways in which God works within us—working into our souls the nature of Jesus, the meek and lowly One (Matthew 11:29, KJV). My prayer is that you will not merely gain more "understanding" about what it means to be a Christian. Understanding will not do it. Instead, my hope is that you will allow God to search the deep places inside—that you will surrender any points of resistance that are keeping you from being at one with the will of the Father. My prayer is that this book will be a tool to help you experience the nature of Christ growing in you.

chapter two

praying as Jesus prayed

"And when He had sent the multitudes away, He went up
on the mountain by Himself to pray. Now when evening
came, He was alone there."—MATTHEW 14:23

IN ATLANTA where I live, people do not like to wait—
especially on the Interstate. The first time I pulled
onto Interstate 285, which circles the city of Atlanta,
I was practically knocked off the road as cars and tractor
trailers went roaring by me. Driving the speed limit, I felt
like a snail, because all the other vehicles were blowing by
at fifteen and twenty miles an hour faster than the law allowed—with no one stopping them. Three times I was cut
off by other drivers dodging into my lane to pass someone
in their own lane. Once an eighteen-wheeler almost flat-
tened me against a cement barrier. And I thought when I

moved into the Deep South that the pace of life would be more mellow!

The truth is, people are people, wherever they are. When it comes to driving habits or our intensity on the Internet, we all want to get things done ASAP—as soon as possible. We eat instant grits. We drink instant coffee. We find the highest-speed Internet connection. As a civilization, I doubt if we could build another Great Wall of China, or the pyramids—or accomplish any of the other great achievements of human ingenuity that required time, deliberation, and a vast master plan. Who would have the patience? Who would want to devote time and energy to a plan that could not be completed in their lifetime? Ridiculous!

As I consider today's fast-paced living, I realize how seriously our addiction to speed has hurt our relationship with God—the One whose plans are vast and deep and often hidden from the hurried eye. As Christians, we set out to develop a regular "prayer time" in our day. But if God doesn't "show up" in the first five minutes, we think, *What's the point? Am I getting anywhere? Why am I doing this?* In ten minutes we're restless . . . and then we're gone. Does that sound familiar?

The reason many of us feel bored and ineffective as Christians, even distant from God, is that we have not cultivated patience in prayer. We have been unwilling to wait long enough to develop a strong, deep connection. We have refused to humble ourselves enough to accept His timetable. We are always pushing to have things done in our way and on our schedule.

Bill has been praying for the success of his business. He's frustrated because in five years his business has not grown, and has even suffered what he would call "definite setbacks." But Bill's prayers, which he offers up in the car on the way to work—in a total of three minutes—go like this: "Make this business a success, Lord, and I'll honor You with the glory for it, and give You bigger offerings." He isn't interested in developing the habit of listening in prayer so that God could actually shine the light on certain attitudes that are preventing his success. Is he growing in the character of Christ? Truthfully, that's hardly a blip on his radar screen.

Shayna is ready to give up on prayer, too. She keeps asking God to change her husband, her children, her annoying sister, and several people at church. If she were to stop, quiet her complaints, and listen, she might hear God's instructions to her—all the attitudes He wants to replace because they keep her rising up and lashing out, rather than letting the love of God be seen in her.

The only relationship these two have with God is that

they are trying to be His "boss." Of course, God needs no boss. Surely, not any one of us. A true relationship with God comes only through learning what it means to mature in prayer. For many of us, it's time to move beyond those childish (also bossy and impatient!) prayers that are all about *asking for something for ourselves and not about offering ourselves to God*. It is time to grow up into the type of prayer that brings our whole life into surrender to God's will. This type of prayer requires the transformation of our very nature. As one saint put it, "To pray is to labor . . . with all possible diligence to bring [our] will into conformity with the will of God."[2]

Often the stock market is on a roller coaster ride, climbing higher than was ever thought possible, or dropping low. People become millionaires or paupers overnight. I know people who watch the Dow and the Nasdaq all day to see how they can cash in and get rich. We need to learn how to pray with that same intensity, because even though there is nothing wrong with worldly wealth, the spiritual riches that are at stake in our prayer lives are of far greater value than anything the stock market has to offer.

If we are ever going to discover real effectiveness in prayer, we will have to go about our praying with the same intensity that we have been giving to our other activities.

We will have to allow God to transform us on the inside until we're able to communicate with Him in the spirit and nature of Jesus Christ.

Humility in Prayer

Christ's attitude of humility will teach us how to approach prayer in the right spirit. It will teach us how to take our place as CEOs in charge of running the world. His humility will qualify us to take a leadership role in world affairs and to have influence over other people's lives. Without humility, we get things confused and out of order and our lives are ineffective, but God's power is released on our behalf when we pray according to His will (1 John 5:14). If we're not in line with God's will, our prayer life will be ineffective. If we are in line, we can accomplish His purposes in the earth.

In Luke's Gospel we read of a time when Jesus sent out His disciples, telling them to preach the Gospel and to demonstrate His power by healing the sick and casting out demons. We can only imagine their excitement—and maybe the little bit of "holy shine" they wore—as they entered those country villages. They thought they would be showing those people the kind of spiritual authority they had! But the demons would not come out at their word.

When they complained to Jesus that their prayers didn't "work," Jesus must have shook His head. To enter into the deep, intense works of God, He told them, required prayer and fasting (see Mark 9:29). Prayer, it is clear, required some sacrifice of them—and it requires something of us. But what does true prayer—prayer that is going to be answered—require of us?

Waiting

First of all, when we pray, we can't be in a hurry. We can't expect God to honor our time, while we do not respect His. That must change. True prayer begins when we are willing to spend time with God on His schedule, not ours.

Jesus sometimes got up "a great while before day" (Mark 1:35), or He spent all night alone just to pray (Luke 6:12). He received His direction from prayer because He quieted Himself to hear the voice of the Father. As the psalmist wrote,

Lord, my heart is not haughty, nor my eyes lofty. Neither do I concern myself with great matters, nor with things too profound for me. Surely I have calmed and quieted my soul, like a weaned child with his mother; like a weaned child is my soul within me —PSALM 131:1, 2.

Our relationship with the Father is not something that we should take lightly. We need to learn to cultivate moments when we can be alone with God, to get up before sunrise, to set aside special places to be alone with Him.

It is foolish to skip prayer to do something "more important." The most important thing you can do *is* to pray. Jesus didn't skip prayer. If *He* needed to pray, and He had been with the Father in heaven before the foundation of the world, how much more is prayer necessary for us!

When e-commerce is hot, business start-ups come along every day. Most copy the methods of other Internet companies they view as successful. What the Church has not seen very clearly is how to copy Jesus. He had the most successful prayer life of all time. He knew how to stay connected to God. When He prayed, things happened. That's the kind of prayer life we need.

We need to learn how to be persistent in prayer—not to get what we want, but to develop our communication link to God. We have to stop being so impatient and demanding about prayer. Would Jesus act up on His Father like that? Then neither should we. It is our impatience that causes many of us to secretly believe that prayer "doesn't work." It does work, and some of its deepest work is *in us*.

Prayer, in the humility of Jesus, requires waiting on God. That does not mean sitting around drumming our fingers waiting for God to do something. Patience is an active process. It is a time of quieting ourselves, a time of waiting in the court of the great King of Kings. We need to spend less time talking and more time actively waiting and listening.

The Hebrew word for "wait" means "to become entwined like a rope." This is what Isaiah meant when he wrote, "But those who wait on the Lord shall renew their strength . . ." (40:31). Waiting on God means becoming entwined with Him and committed to His purposes, no matter how long it takes. Building a relationship like that gives us inner strength, and it is a life work. God's schedule is rarely the same as ours. "He has made everything beautiful in its time," the writer of Ecclesiastes reminded us. "Also He has put eternity in their hearts, except that no one can find out the work that God does from beginning to end" (Ecclesiastes 3:11).

His Time, His Agenda

As we spend time waiting before God, we begin to put into practice one simple truth: Our time belongs to the Lord of our lives. His timetable is different from ours. So are his plans and his ways of accomplishing them. "For as the heavens are higher than the earth, so are My ways higher than your ways, and My thoughts than your thoughts" (Isaiah 55:9).

When we toss off hasty prayers, refusing to wait on God for a response, it is almost always because we believe *we* know what needs to be done . . . and when . . . and how. Why wait? Often, we are very wrong.

Several years ago, as I saw how people were responding to the word that God had given me when I was interviewed on Christian television, I thought that I should find a way to teach more regularly on national TV. However, my spiritual father, Jay Grimstead, cautioned me to wait. He said it was not quite my time yet, and I should wait on God a little longer. How right he was. As I concentrated on prayer and pastoring my church in Richmond, Virginia, and then responded to requests to travel and speak nationally, God taught me much more that I needed to know, and in the process *He* began to bring my ministry to the attention of national leaders. By waiting, I allowed God to make the moves His way.

Augustine, the Church father and theological giant of the fourth century, understood that true prayer begins as we set aside our own agendas to listen, and to wait. He warned that those in the Church who only know how to ask God for what *they* want have a weak faith. He referred to this as an "Ishmael" kind of faith, because it never leads us to the kind of relationship with God where we rise above our earthly needs and come to understand His mind and heart. If we don't understand. *His* goals, we will not be alert enough in spirit to recognize when they are fulfilled. "Ishmael therefore was in darkness, Isaac in light."[3]

Waiting on God is the first step in giving up our agendas, our plans, our ways, so we can hear His voice. Quite simply, waiting gives us time to realize and acknowledge the presence of another Person as we listen for His voice. Brother Lawrence was a seventeenth-century French monk whose life of simplicity and devotion to God has become a model for many generations. It was said "that his prayer was nothing else but a sense of the presence of God."[4] The goal of prayer is to have fellowship with our Lord, because fellowship is the attitude of life in which we need to walk every day.

The "other Person" in prayer is not just another friend, He is *Lord*. It is His agenda that is important, not ours. He is weaving together the circumstances of our lives—yes, even the tribulations and trials—into something we cannot see. He has a plan for us beyond our understanding. That is why we can say that prayer is more than just a time to receive "marching orders." It is the way we draw closer to understand the heart of the Father.

Perhaps one of the clearest insights into this truth is Jesus' prayer in the Garden of Gethsemane. In the hours before He was to be arrested and crucified, enduring the wrenching loneliness of seeming abandonment by His

Father, Jesus prayed with intensity, "Father, if it is possible, let this cup pass from me" (Matthew 26:39). Though we cannot understand this prayer as fully as it was prayed, we do sense that Christ was looking for the possibility of a way out—another way to accomplish the redemption of the world.

Yet, in the end, Jesus did not resist God's will. He knew His Father's heart. They shared a perfect unity, a perfect love (see John 17:23). That is why Jesus could say to His Father, "[N]evertheless, not my will, but yours be done" (Luke 22:42). In this humility, Jesus could submit Himself even to death on the cross. He knew God had a plan and a purpose that could only be realized through His humility. The relationship He had with the Father helped Jesus stay focused on the joy while He endured the pain (Hebrews 12:2).

In the relationship of prayer—the steady practice of God's presence—God teaches us how to give up our concerns and worries so we can hear His voice. Giving our cares to God is one of the steps that leads us to a lifestyle of fellowship—even intimacy. It is an important means that God uses to train us to surrender ourselves to Him. We learn to yield to God not because we are forced, but because of love.

Intimacy

Some Christians recoil at the idea of intimacy with God. It sounds too emotionally enmeshed, or too sexual, like a modern film scene. But to be intimate in the biblical sense means to know someone's mind thoroughly . . . and more than that, their very spirit. The same biblical word for knowing God is used for intimate intercourse—not only in the sense of physical contact but also in the sense of that very private relationship that exists between a husband and wife who have developed a sincere heart for one another.

One story is told of a wealthy young plantation owner in Rhode Island during the time of slavery. His family had made their fortune farming, using African slave labor. The young man's father was away in Europe on extended business and personal travels when Quaker preachers came through New England, preaching against the evils of slavery. The young man was so deeply touched, and converted, that he knew his family could no longer make their living off the toil of other human beings. In fact, he knew he couldn't bear to hold slaves for even the few months it would take for his father to return home. Immediately, he gave the slaves their freedom, a bold act that earned him the disapproval of his father's friends. Many, thinking he had committed an unpardonable offense, were sure his father would disinherit him and counseled their own sons to avoid his example.

When the young man's father returned, their first meeting, at the front gate, was a charged moment. "Father," he said, "I have become convinced slavery is altogether evil. And so I have acted—perhaps in some haste—but I have set them all free."

At first, the father was furious. But as the son opened the Scriptures to him, about God's intense love for men of every race and nation, the father became convicted, too. In a short time, he was weeping.

"Son, the greatness of your heart puts me to shame," he said. "You saw this evil before my wicked heart would allow me to see it. And moreover, you risked all not knowing but I might turn you out and cut you off from our fortune without a penny."

"Not so great as all that, father," the son replied. "I acted as I did only because I knew your heart."

That is intimacy. As we submit our time and agendas to God in prayer, true intimacy with God takes place. That is because submission breaks the old controlling nature—the self-willed nature—and makes us ready to come in line with God's will, enabled to receive His strength and joy for the journey of becoming Christ-like.

Of course, God does not mind if we speak to Him about our lives, our needs, and our dreams. He is our Father! What loving daddy does not like for his children to come sit on his lap and tell him what's on their hearts? This is certainly part of our relationship with our heavenly Father, too. Yet we sometimes confuse the lap of a father with the lap of a department store Santa Claus. No good father gives a child everything he wants. Some of the things we asked for as children were not in our best interest. Even as Jesus told us to ask for our daily needs, He also began to instruct us about the proper asking attitude: "Do not worry about your life," Jesus said. "Your heavenly Father knows that you need all these things. But seek first the kingdom of God and His righteousness, and all these things shall be added to you" (Matthew 6:25, 33).

Power

I use the words "power in prayer" advisedly. If we think that we will somehow develop our praying to the point where it is some sort of spiritual skill, giving us the ability to direct God's power wherever we will, we are headed in the wrong direction. Simon the sorcerer saw God's hand move to heal a lame beggar through the apostles Peter and John, and he offered them gold in exchange for this power (see Acts 8:18–24). Peter rebuked him: "Your money perish with you" (Acts 8:20).

The power of God that we witness in prayer is never *our* power. To believe we can direct God's power in prayer is a serious mistake and an offense against God. Our place is always, and only, the place of a servant who is directed by God in our praying as well as in our life of service to Him. In fact, the power comes *because* we are God's servants carrying out His plan. The power is simply the provision.

One man who often comes to mind when I think about trusting God for provision and power is George Mueller. Three weeks after he was married, he and his wife had made decisions to launch a ministry to orphans and be totally dependent on the Father, never asking anyone but God to support them. More than a century ago, they started several orphanages in England, and through prayer saw miracles of God's provision again and again. By the time the Lord called George Mueller home, they had seen God support the ministries through prayer alone for 68 years. During that time, God supplied for those children about $7.5 million—an incredible sum in that day.

The Muellers' mission was highly successful, but there did come a test. At one point, with hundreds of mouths to feed, there was no money. Mueller had always hidden his needs from the staff. He felt it was his duty alone.

However, he came to realize that his legalism in not making his needs known was robbing them of the blessing of giving and praying for results. Humiliated, he broke to his staff the news of their lack. There was no money to pay them their salary, and no money for food for the orphans. But instead of seeing them walk out, he saw them begin to empty their pockets, giving him everything they had!

One of those workers was a widow. On the spot, she was moved by God to renounce all compensation from the ministries, insisting she would live only on the money from her small pension. Another gave the little nest egg she was saving in the bank. When their small offerings were used up to feed the orphans, people began slipping quietly out of the building carrying parcels, which Mueller found out later were their own possessions that they were taking out to sell so they could give a few shillings more. They told him they had discovered what an awesome thing it was to give, and they wanted to experience the intimacy of joining God in his compassionate work for these homeless boys and girls.

Like George Mueller, as we pray in humility, we ourselves are humbled. As we spend time with the Creator of the universe, we find ourselves being re-created, renewed, "transformed into the image that we reflect in brighter and brighter glory" (2 Corinthians 3:18, New Jerusalem Bible).

God's power is released not only to change us, but to change others as well. That is God's plan. And when Christ's humble Spirit shapes our prayers, we will begin to long for the lost of the world to come to God and be saved.

Revival

From the outset, I have acknowledged that this book is being offered with the sense that God wants to bring revival. Revival must begin in our hearts, in prayer. God needs men and women who will wait on Him in prayer and then humbly go out and do whatever the Holy Spirit tells them.

Too often we hear of "miracles" being done here or there and we are tempted to think "Revival!" But miraculous evidences of God's power can so easily become a distraction, taking our eyes off the worship of God Himself. We like God to "do" for us. What He wants is to live in us, and through us, to reach all of His lost children.

We cannot be the instruments of revival unless we first have died to ourselves. It is only when we acknowledge our weakness before God that we can receive others who are weak. We are then able to understand what Jesus was trying to impress upon the seventy He had sent out: We should rejoice not in the privilege of God's power for its own sake, but that He uses His power to save us and others. He does the impossible. He sets us free.

God freed black Americans when they were slaves. They couldn't do it on their own. Yes, America fought a Civil War—but the real war was won in heaven through the people's prayers. When the war was over and the slaves were freed, those people who had endured such hardship and humiliation were incredibly strong Christians. One man, C. H. Mason, founder of the Church of God in Christ, was propelled forward into his great worldwide ministry through the prayers he heard coming from the lips of his parents and other former slaves. He wanted above all else to have their kind of faith, a faith that held on—persevering in humility—until thousands upon thousands were finally set free. That is the ministry of Jesus that we are called to follow.

Intercession

Right now—all the time—Jesus is meeting with the Father on our behalf. He never stops praying for us. In fact, He intercedes for the whole world. To intercede means "to intervene on someone's behalf." Jesus intervened on our behalf when He died on the cross, taking the punishment for our sins. With His resurrection, He intervened again, securing the promise of eternal life. Now, seated at the right hand of his Father, He continues that ministry. "He is . . . able to save to the uttermost those who come to God through Him, since He always lives to make intercession for them" (Hebrews 7:25).

Revival will mean that many, many people will come to the throne of grace. Some of those people we will like. Some we will not. But if we have remained humble, thankful that our slavery was ended through the intercession of Christ, we will also be willing to intercede through Christ on their behalf. And we will continue to intercede, long past the decision "for salvation," to see our new brothers and sisters continue to grow in the knowledge and love of our Lord and Savior Jesus Christ.

We will know that the nature of Jesus Christ, the lowly, is growing in us when prayer is no longer a "hurried demand"—when instead, we see our hearts change so that we carry in us, like a cross, the desire to see those in our world reconciled to God.

chapter three

a bridge
to be
walked on

"And a main road will go through that once deserted
land. It will be named the Highway of Holiness."
—ISAIAH 35:8, TLB

I HAVE A HARD TIME with all this talk about 'inner
transformation' and 'growing in humility,' " Alec admits. "In fact, it irritates me. It seems as if we're
weakening the Gospel. Talking about 'becoming like Jesus'
is well and good, but there's a battle being fought in our
culture today between good and evil. And if we spend all
our time mucking around in our souls, hoping to become
gentle and humble like Jesus, being 'nice,' we're going to
become weaklings who lose the war."

Lisa's concern is different. "No one could ever measure
up to Jesus. He was perfect. Didn't God send Jesus to be

our *perfect* Savior, and the *perfect* sacrifice for our sins? Didn't He show us an example of perfection to convince us how wretched and *imperfect* we are? People will never be perfect. All we can do is try to do the best we can."

Alec and Lisa have voiced two of the main misunderstandings that prevent many Christians today from growing into the character and nature of Christ. They represent two prevailing attitudes:

- The first attitude might be called "bottom-line Christianity." It could be stated this way: "All we need to do is know God's Word, then we go out and do it." It's simple, just trust and obey—right? When you listen to bottom-liners like Alec—and there are many like him these days—you might think that God's main agenda item reads: "Just get the job done. Don't get all involved with that spiritual self-examination stuff."
- The second attitude might be called "a Christianity of excuses." People who see Jesus as perfect and themselves as imperfect think they have the perfect excuse for sloppy *agape*.* They don't have to try too hard to

---

* *Agape*, the Greek word for unconditional love, is "sloppy" when people think that God loves them so much He will not force them to change their ways or to set higher standards for themselves. They lack an understanding of His perfect holiness.

change, because they will never be like Jesus anyway. This sense of imperfection may give them inner conflicts of unworthiness, but more often it gives them an arrogance that says that they don't have to change.

Recently, a group of people began to picket one of several abortion clinics run by the same doctor. Every day, she had to make her way through lines of protesters, claiming to be Christians—all chanting slogans. Some referred to her as "murderer" and "baby killer." Since they were not on her property, and didn't assault her physically, there was nothing she could do to stop the protest. But she felt assaulted in spirit, and bitter toward these "self-righteous" people. She didn't have any time for them and their God, let alone their conservative social agenda.

During the many months that this protest went on, the doctor complained over and over to a close friend. The friend, another woman, listened patiently as the doctor began to speak about her own, deep, spiritual questions, as well as personal struggles and needs. Eventually, the friend revealed that she was a Christian—and not only that, but she had been praying for her for a long time. The disclosure might have killed the friendship, because the doctor was pretty tired of people who called themselves Christians and who judged her—but something in her friend's demeanor would not let her end the relationship. What was so different about her?

Not long after, the doctor committed her life to Christ. Her conversion was a shock to her local medical community and to Christians, too. She stopped performing abortions. What was it that turned the key to open her heart? "I saw the humbleness of Christ in my friend," she admits. "She never came on strong, telling me she was right and I was wrong. She loved me, and waited patiently for God to give her an opening . . . and then give her the right words to say to me."

In this example, we can readily see how waiting on God, in the humility of Christ, is not the weak road. This is not to say that those who were protesting in the streets were not involved in the work of God, but what this Christian woman did for her friend was more effective for her personally. It required great strength in Spirit, character, patience—and above all, absolute trust in God—not to speak out so strongly about her friend's sin that she never reached her heart.

The second attitude, which we saw at work in Lisa, might be stated this way: "God is so utterly holy, and so powerful, He doesn't need unclean wretches like us to do anything for Him. And besides that, anything we could do for Him would be puny and fairly useless."

To those like Lisa, who feel that God just *tolerates* us but doesn't expect too much of us, I would say that this kind of thinking gives us an unholy attitude that causes us to hold back from simply trusting in God's love and His ability to change us into the image of His Son. It makes us constantly self-examining, always putting ourselves down for not being good enough or making excuses for not growing up, so we get reduced down in our estimation of where we should be as Christians.

With both of the attitudes described here, we wind up out of balance. When we take charge of God's work, we rush ahead of God, muscling our way through. In the end we may destroy something of the fine work of the Spirit within other people. When we focus on ourselves and our imperfections, we deny that the power of God can work through vessels like us and we lag behind. In the end, God's work in the world is left undone, while we polish and repolish our own souls.

The apostle Peter spoke of the attitude of heart that leads us into the spiritual balance we need: "Humble yourselves, therefore, under God's mighty hand, that He may lift you up in due time" (1 Peter 5:6). To find spiritual balance you must first wait, and listen, and yield your will to God's will. And then, second, you must watch expectantly for God to lift you up and set you in place for the work that

He has chosen for you. *We go low; He lifts us and puts us in place.* In this way, we allow God to weave us into the fabric of His great work.

Reconciliation

Paul tells us that "God . . . reconciled us to Himself through Jesus Christ, . . . reconciling the world to Himself" (2 Corinthians 5:18, 19). Paul also tells us that God gave us the ministry of reconciliation (v. 18). God's great work was, and is, to close the gulf that exists between the people of this world and Himself. In this work, we are His "ambassadors," and it's "as though God [Himself] were making His appeal through us" (v. 20, NIV).

Jesus, of course, was the Chief Ambassador. He was the first and main span in the great bridge God built so that mankind could cross the cosmic gulf and come to His side as His children. As we learn to wait upon God in prayer, listening for His instructions, we begin to understand the work He wants to do in the lives of people all around us. If we assume we know what needs to be done, we are often wrong. Like Christ, we need to lay down our understanding with our lives, so that we can become a bridge that someone can walk on to God. If you have enough character to let people walk on you—rather than rising up to knock them down—they will be able to get to God through the ministry of Christ in you.

Rejection

Being a bridge means being selfless and serving—whether others appreciate it or not. Jesus said to "love your enemies, do good to them which hate you, bless them that curse you, and pray for them which despitefully use you" (Luke 6:27–28, KJV). He wants us to give them a chance to walk on us to get to the Savior. When we can bless those who curse us, and do good to those who use us, then there is a power that comes through in our weakness. Most people have never have met anybody who will put up with their stubbornness long enough to help them find their way to God.

One of the most prolific and gifted preachers in history was the nineteenth century's Charles Spurgeon. Even as a young man preaching in London, he attracted large crowds. Some called him "the prince of preachers." Spurgeon's preaching was so powerful that in an age where other churches were losing members, he preached to thousands every week. And he always preached a message of salvation. As he put it, "I take my text and make a bee-line to the cross."

But Spurgeon was also called a few less savory names than "prince of preachers" throughout his forty years of ministry. Like Jesus, he knew what it was to be despised and rejected. Along with that, he was troubled by many serious physical ailments and suffered from long, unexplainable bouts of depression. What gave Spurgeon his power, however, was this: As a young man, he learned how to die to himself so that his message would not be hindered by his pride or by natural limitations. Late in life, looking back on the death-to-self experience of those early years, he said,

> If I am able to say in very truth, "I was buried with Christ thirty years ago," I must surely be dead. Certainly the world thought so, for not long after my burial with Jesus I began to preach his name, and by that time the world thought me very far gone, and said, "He stinketh." They began to say all manner of evil against the preacher; but the more I stank in their nostrils the better I liked it, for the surer I was that I was really dead to the world.[5]

Spurgeon exhibited Christ-like humility when faced with continuing attacks from his enemies, and he did so by laying down pride and defensiveness. In this way, the strength of Christ became apparent in him. He wrote,

Down on my knees have I often fallen, with the hot
sweat rising from my brow, under some fresh slander
poured upon me, in an agony of grief my heart has been
well-nigh broken; . . . this thing I hope I can say from
my heart: if to be made as the mire of the streets again,
if to be the laughing stock of fools and the song of the
drunkard once more will make me more serviceable to
my Master, and more useful to his cause, I will prefer it
to all this multitude, or to all the applause that man
could give.[6]

Spurgeon knew something about the work of reconciliation that we need to know. Like Christ, he learned to let
himself be criticized without striking back, and he learned
how to bear his own infirmities with patience. So he became a man who could change his generation.

Take a moment to examine your life. Are there any areas
of immaturity where you waste time agonizing over what
others think and say about you? With God's grace, we need
to test our level of spiritual maturity in Christ from time to
time. How do we do this?

Consider the way you handled your last misunderstand-
ing with someone who offended you. Did you give in and
get angry? Did you go away hurt and pout? Did you rise up
in self-defense and verbally shoot him down? Or did you
remain still and patient? Did you give him a living,

breathing example, as God's ambassador of reconciliation, of the way our Father welcomes even His enemies?

There are times when I've encountered racists. They have a problem with my color. I'm an "undesirable" to them, and yet they claim to be Christians. If I have not surrendered my own hostility and prejudice against racists, there is no way God can use me to help them overcome their inner conflicts and come to God.

Let's dwell on this point for just a moment. What we in the minority communities need to realize is this: For a man to enslave or put down another person, he has to be very insecure. If I am a threat to someone, God can use me—if I lay my needs and my pride aside—to help him overcome his insecurity and fear. Do you see? We can't hate someone and help him at the same time. We are called to love those who hate us, because that is how we win them to God in Christ.

As a closing thought on this particular issue, I must say this, as well. In many churches in the black community, we have developed a social gospel that has replaced the preaching of the cross. I understand we have done so because we are being sympathetic to people's suffering. People grow weary of mistreatment by others, but too often we focus on what our pride tells us we deserve, to the exclusion of God's right to do whatever He pleases with our lives. Following Jesus means following His work of reconciliation. That means we are to love our neighbors—*and* our enemies—as ourselves.

This is a hard teaching to hear. I understand that. That is because the essence of reconciliation is death—laying aside our rights in the way Jesus laid aside His rights. To become a reconciler in the humble nature of Jesus is to lay aside our rights. It is to lay aside all that inner disturbance that comes when we feel violated, in order to let the peace of God rule in our hearts. That is when we begin to become an ambassador of God—when His peace in us becomes an offering of peace to others.

Jesus laid aside His rights as God when He came as a man (see Philippians 2) to save us. He also demonstrated a lifestyle of laying aside His rights with His disciples. At the Last Supper, He laid aside His garment and began to wash their feet (see John 13:3–15).

He "laid aside His garments, took a towel and girded Himself. After that, He poured water into a basin and began to wash the disciples' feet, and to wipe them with the towel with which He was girded" (John 13:4–5). He washed Peter's feet, even though Peter resisted Him. He washed Judas's feet, even though he knew Judas would betray him. And He said, "Do you know what I have done to you? You call me Teacher and Lord, and you say well, for so

I am. If I then, your Lord and Teacher, have washed your feet, you also ought to wash one another's feet. For I have given you an example, that you should do as I have done to you" (John 13:12–15).

But!

Is something rising up in you now? Is there a voice saying, "But what about justice? Fairness? Equality? What about righting wrongs? Isn't this just 'Uncle Tom' kind of talk?" In no way am I saying that we pretend we don't see wrongs, whether in racial issues or in any other venue of life. But I am saying that our first responsibility is to get our own attitudes right, and then listen to God for His direction concerning the work we are called to do—and what we are not called to do.

Reconciliation is His work. His throne is established in mercy (Isaiah 16:5). Passing judgment is his "strange work" (Isaiah 28:21, KJV). Vengeance belongs to God. He is counting on us to be instruments of His mercy, like Jesus. Being like Jesus requires a death—our death. "While we were yet sinners, Christ died for us" (Romans 5:8, KJV). This is the bottom line. We need to let God be God in our lives. We need to restore Him to His rightful place as the righteous judge, and we need to take our place behind

Him as He leads us on the path of reconciliation—laying down our offenses and our pride so that others can see the peace and love of God in us.

Let me ask: Who is provoking you so seriously that you want just one opportunity to put him in his place so that you can feel satisfied? The problem is that the desire for retribution is never satisfied. The one who is offending you is someone God is asking you to love and bring to salvation. The one who torments you today will thank you in heaven one day.

When we become Christians, when we say we're willing to become like Christ, we must ask Him to train us until we know how to bear offenses as He did. Only He can help us bear with patience the abuses that we never anticipated. Only He can show us how to love those who use us wrongly.

A few years ago, I moved from Richmond, Virginia, to Atlanta, Georgia, because of a specific word from the Lord. It was the first time I had ever experienced anything that strong. I told our staff and the members of my church about it, and eventually about seventy-five families made the move with me. We started an Atlanta church with one of my associates as the pastor under me.

While I was traveling, my associate decided privately that he and his wife would really like to be in charge of the church. Not only that, but they would like to run the campus ministry that I had founded many years earlier. I gave it all to him, blessed him, and went and started another church with twelve people and raised up a whole new campus ministry.

He was not just another pastor to me. He was my son. He had been with me for years, ever since his college days, but he turned away, and I decided that the Christ-like thing was to let him go, taking everything that we had worked on together, while I went down into the ground for a while. I don't wish him anything bad. I want him to be successful. I told him to "use me," and I know that he uses my name to get in places where he might not otherwise go. I told him to do that, and I hope that God will bless him.

We Stand Before God Alone

When you begin to follow Jesus in this work of reconciliation, I can tell you that even the Christian crowd starts to thin out around you. At the end, when Jesus was left to die on the cross, no one was there for Him. He suffered alone. Though He had many followers, few proved to be true disciples—much less friends. When the pressure was on, they bailed out. Jesus knew about the fickleness of man. He knows what is in us and that we are only dust. But Jesus' disciples took their eyes off Him. They stopped watching

Him and so they stopped following what He was doing as He laid down His life. Even the one disciple who was confident he would never leave Jesus failed at first.

Peter was certain he would not deny Jesus, but he did. Out of pride he lashed out with a sword (John 18:10). Then he cursed when someone said they had seen him with Jesus. Sometimes we are like Peter. We claim to be followers of Christ, but our fear and anger drive us to do things our way. We have little substance in our souls, and the reality of our faith is shallow.

Saints with Substance

We are not alone in our "lite" variety of faith. The Western Church in this generation has lost its willingness to sacrifice. How many people do you know who can fast even one meal a week? How many will go as missionaries into the hard places to bring God's message of reconciliation? Who is going to the inner cities right down the street to take the light of the Gospel?

It's sad to say, but in America, especially, the Church is becoming little more than an entertainment medium. Sometimes in our zeal to try to attract "a new crowd" with flashier music and better programs, we become weak as water. It's time for the Church to develop saints with substance who are willing to lay down their lives, who are committed to reaching people, regardless of the personal cost, and become spans in the bridge of reconciliation to God.

There are Christians today who say this cannot be done, that the Church of this generation is too far gone. That is faithlessness. At the wedding in Cana, Jesus told the servants to bring Him large jugs of water, then take the water to the master of the banquet (John 2:1–11). By the time the water reached the master it was wine, the best wine, saved for last. In the same way, we need to ask God to change our "weak-water" spirit into the wine of the Holy Spirit.

People of Love

We have been referring to the bridge that God is building, using His Son Jesus first, and also those who will lay down their lives as He did, to let people walk on them. God wants us to widen this bridge until it's a highway on which the people of this world come flooding to Him. Listen to what God had to say through the prophet Isaiah:

And a main road will go through that once deserted land. It will be named the Highway of Holiness. Evil-hearted people will never travel on it. It will be only for those who walk in God's ways; fools will never walk there. Lions will not lurk along its course, and there will be no other dangers. Only the redeemed will follow it. Those who have been ransomed by the Lord will return to Jerusalem, singing songs of everlasting joy. Sorrow and mourning will disappear, and they will be overcome with joy and gladness—ISAIAH 35:8–10, TLB.

The first thing we are promised as we become the highway on which others come to God is "songs of everlasting joy." We were created to know the joy that lasts for eternity. That joy comes as we set ourselves aside, and lay down our lives for others. There are many today who think this idea is insane and self-martyring. But those who walk this path with Christ quickly find a different truth. By discovering how much God values those who do not yet know Him, we discover our own value in reaching them for Him.

We are the valued friends of God when we do what He asks us to do (John 15:14). When we love as God loves, when we lay ourselves down for another, we can never lose our sense of value. We serve and maintain our dignity because we know who we are in Christ. We are then bridge builders for God.

The Bible tells us that Jesus washed His disciples' feet (John 13:5). What motivated Him, if not love? Jesus not only loved His friends and wanted to refresh them, He also wanted to show them how to serve God by loving and serving one another. He wanted to show them that this type of loving humility gives us great value in the eyes of the Father. Rising up and demanding our way will never bring us the joy and fulfillment we find by laying aside our desires and serving God by serving others.

My Prayer for You

Lord, I am not satisfied with where I am when there is so much more of You that You can give. I am asking You, out of an intensity of spirit that You have given me, to come upon us, Lord. Don't let us just talk about the revivals of old and what You have done in the past to bring reconciliation. For this is the day that You have made. Don't let us be an embarrassment to You. Don't let us compare ourselves any longer to other Christians whom we know, those whom we may even perceive as being serious. But let us see Your face and get Your approval and get Your rebuke and Your intentions, so that You can bring the transformation necessary for us to do the job in this hour, through the help of the Holy Spirit.

Break the yoke of racial distinctions. Help us to know that we can be culturally conscious but not culturally controlled. Help us to become masters of self-control. Where cities have been known for negativism in the past, restore the places that have become desolate. Let the stumbling blocks of the past become stepping stones to a new move of God and to a new intensity to see You move.

Raise up the churches. Give them the spirit to be serious. In these latter days, let them be the latter rain, my Father, that comes upon the earth before the harvest of souls in this generation. Open the floodgates of heaven. Pour out Your Spirit upon us. Don't let us be like Jerusalem, where You said the city would be laid to the ground because they didn't discern the hour of Your visitation. Cause us to discern that there is something stirring. There is something in the heart of the Lord. There is something in the Holy Ghost. There is a move coming. Don't let us talk about running away from the trouble, but let us talk about something that You are stirring inside of us to go to the trouble.

Let every person say with conviction, "Lord, use me." Let them not just look to someone else who is being used, but let them say in their own hearts, "Use me even if no one else will be used." Grant that, Lord, I pray, in Jesus' name. Amen.

chapter four

fathering the future

"For though you might have ten thousand instructors in
Christ, yet you do not have many fathers; for in Christ
Jesus I have begotten you through the gospel."
—1 CORINTHIANS 4:15

MANY CHRISTIAN LEADERS believe America
is poised for another Great Awakening, like
those witnessed in the eighteenth and nineteenth centuries. Wholesale, people turned their lives
over to the worship and service of God. Others are saying
that America will not experience revival in this generation, that revival will be blocked by sin. By that, they mean
the sexual promiscuity promoted by the media, the fraud
that goes on at all levels of business, government corruption, and the utter disrespect of human life that is making
us a violent society. You can also add to that the disregard
for the poor and elderly, along with hatred for minorities.

While I agree that these are great sins, I do not agree that these sins alone—terrible as they are—can hold back the revival I believe God wants to bring in our day. But one sin can. That is the sin of pride that causes rebellion among God's own people. The sin of insisting on our own way, which leads to discord, infighting, churches in constant upheaval, and split after split in the body of Christ. For we are God's vessels of spiritual awakening—and what is that, first and foremost, but the recognition of the Father's authority and sovereign, loving government over us all?

Brothers and sisters in Christ, what God means to accomplish in the world He must accomplish in us first. Revival, like judgment, begins at the house of the Lord (see 1 Peter 4:17). So the question is not "Is the world ready for revival?" The question is "Are *we*?"

Heart of the Problem

At the heart of a spiritual revival beats a revived awareness of God's loving but very definite authority over our lives. Today, we mistake emotion and so-called "fervor" for revival, but that may be nothing more than excitement and soul heat. The first step on the road to true revival is a time of mourning and repentance for sin. If you consider the great biblical revivals, such as the one in Nehemiah's time, you will quickly see that God's directives became of prime importance again—to the extent that men were even willing, despite what they felt, to dismiss the idol-worshipping, heathen wives they had married when they were in rebellion against God's explicit prohibition of this act (see Ezra 9, 10).

If we want revival, we must first renew our commitment to obey Him, regardless of the cost. True revival always results in a new dedication to do His will. Obedience, not necessarily emotion, lies at its core. And in order for us to embrace that obedience in a personal way, we must become willing to submit ourselves, body, mind, and soul, to the Father. We must be open to correction. Most of us, however, do not like correction, do we? We never have. That is truly our problem. We do not want to be opposed, challenged, or directed by anybody but us. The right to be independent, to choose our own destiny, we hold as our greatest right. Because it is part and parcel of Western culture, it has seeped into the Western Church.

But do you realize that the worst thing that can ever happen to us is for God to leave us alone so we can go our own way without Him? Many of us want God to be "somewhere" in our lives—close enough so that we can call Him and He'll come running when we're scared or we need Him, but we do not want Him meddling in our affairs too deeply. We certainly do not want Him taking charge! When most of us "surrendered" our lives to God what we meant was "Here are the messed-up and unhappy parts. Please fix them." We did not mean "Here is my will, the very core of me. Please take it and shape it to your will, so I can be like you and do what you would do."

In a park one beautiful day, a little boy of about four was trying to fly a kite in the light wind while his dad sat nearby coaching him. The kite would soar for a few minutes, then spin out of control and crash to the ground. The father got up each time and tried patiently to teach his son how to get the kite to rise and stay up. But as soon as he got the kite into the air, the little boy grabbed the string and pushed his dad away, saying, "Give me the string. Let me do it. Go sit down."

All the father's instructions were drowned out by his son's impatient demands. He was convinced he could make that kite fly—even though to the mature observer it was clear he didn't have a clue how to do it . . . and he sure wasn't willing to be quiet and learn. You could just about predict how this was going to end.

Shortly, the wind picked up a bit and the kite started to spin and dive. It headed for trees, and then ditched right into the middle of some picnickers on a blanket who had to roll away to avoid injury. At this point the dad became more insistent. "Son, let me help you. You're going to ruin the kite . . . or hurt someone."

But when he took hold of the string, the little boy, who was now frustrated by his own failures, began to shout and cry. "No! No! Let me do it by myself. I can do it."

"Son," said the patient daddy, "let me show you how. Let's do this together."

Throwing himself on the ground, the little boy pitched a fit. Kicking. Screaming. *"Let me do it!"* he shouted over and over, refusing his father's instruction.

In the end, the man had to hoist the little boy off the ground, pack in the kite, and call it a day.

Isn't this a sad but accurate picture of the way we act toward God? We want freedom and fun. We want to hold the string ourselves, even when we clearly do not know what we're doing, even if we're in danger of harming other people. Not only that, we get frustrated and upset by our own failures. And yet, we *still* insist on calling all the shots. It's our right! We do not want God telling us what to do, but God knows patient training and guidance is what we need.

A willingness to submit to God's direction is what we need, if we are going to say with any truthfulness that God is our Father, the One who lovingly shapes and directs our lives. To have the willing, obedient spirit of a child is to have the humble spirit of Christ. If we are lacking this at a core level, how can God use us to tell others how to live as His son or daughter?

Spiritual Fathering

It's clear that Christians need training in what it means to be a willingly obedient child of the Father. But here we meet another problem in the Western Church: a lack of spiritual fathering, by which we are trained in the humility of Christ.

Many Christians are unwilling to submit to our spiritual fathers for training in Christ-likeness. Many do not understand what this even means, and moreover, we lack examples of good spiritual fathers. We prefer relationships in which we are equal, nondemanding partners. We can deal with this arrangement because we can take advice or leave it, but the moment a spiritual leader tries to give us strong direction, watch out! I often challenge Christians with this question: Do you make your pastor want to quit the ministry? I believe that many pastors' hearts are broken because they have a burden to raise up spiritual children in the nature of Christ. But many of us spend our lives like that little boy in the park, demanding our own way, stuck on our own opinions, and so the one we call "pastor"—which means "shepherd"—cannot lead us.

Jeremiah was a frustrated spiritual shepherd who wept for the proud people of His day. Could His words also apply to us?

> Hear ye, and give ear; be not proud: for the LORD hath spoken. Give glory to the LORD your God . . . But if ye will not hear it, my soul shall weep in secret places for your pride; and mine eye shall weep sore, and run down with tears, because the LORD's flock is carried away captive—JEREMIAH 13:15–17, KJV.

Many of us view those in leadership the way the children of Israel viewed Moses. We may not say this openly, but the words are written all over our faces: "Who made you ruler and judge over us?" (Exodus 2:14, NIV).

The plain fact is, we don't want other people to tell us what to do because we think of them as *only* people and do not respect the Spirit of God in them. Rather, people have to impress us with credentials before we will listen to them. Jesus said, "Verily I say unto you, Whosoever shall not receive the kingdom of God as a little child, he shall not enter therein. And he took them up in his arms, put his hands upon them, and blessed them" (Mark 10:15–16, KJV). Many in the Church today are not experiencing the blessing of God's hands upon their lives because they are not allowing themselves, like little children, to be fully directed—that is, to recognize that God's government of our lives will come to us through people whom He places ahead of us in experience and wisdom, and over us in authority. Jesus spiritually trained the people in His care. He was with them on a day-to-day basis, teaching them how to trust God in everything and how to stay in step with His Spirit.

When our pride and self-insistence remain unbroken and we refuse to be discipled, it is often because of our own rebellion and sin. We do not like to be told to stop doing those forbidden things! On the other hand, we are sometimes hard-pressed to find ourselves a spiritual father who is willing to submit to God and lead us.

If we are all so busy straining against each other—resisting leadership, refusing correction—how can we imagine we're ready to submit to the directives of God that must come before we see revival in our time? For revival will come only when we surrender utterly, willingly, joyfully to the authority of God, which will demonstrate to others how to do so. Then our lives and our words will carry authority. We receive authority to the degree that we are under authority.

It is my firm conviction, in these lawless times, that spiritual revival is dependent upon our coming to grips with root issues like respect for leaders in our churches.

The honor we give to God is seen in the honor we give to those in spiritual authority over us, for they are His representatives. If we cannot handle their correction, we will surely never be able to handle the deep-heart corrections that come to us by God's Spirit as He convicts us of sin (John 16:8) and directs us from within. God's Word, to be effective, must penetrate the deepest parts of our life, discerning the thoughts and intents of our heart (Hebrews 4:12–13). If we want revival, personal as well as national, we need to go into the "prayer closet"—wherever we can find a secret place of prayer—and ask God to show us the areas of our lives where we are not surrendered to Him and to those others who can speak for Him into our lives.

Underneath all of our resistance, of course, lies *pride*. When all is said and done, we want to believe we are good, fine, and all right just the way we are, thank you. How can anyone, including God, dare to tell us we are not perfectly right and mature just the way we are?

"Reproof" is a good Bible word and it means to "improve." When we don't like correction, we will not grow. A child who cannot take suggestions for improvement becomes obstinate and unchanging, and will never mature. Because he or she will not yield to what is right, the truth cannot change them. Pride will never give place to true authority, and a willful child—or an immature adult—presupposes that the one bringing correction doesn't know what they are talking about. They think, *I know what is best for me.* Yet God has set people in place over us by virtue of their experience, wisdom, insight, and example of godliness, and they can be a tremendous blessing to us, if we make our hearts teachable and pliable to the truths they bring.

Do we recognize the wonderful system God has put in place, in our homes and in our churches? As the child obeys the parent, the child is changed by what the parent knows. By heeding God's wisdom as it comes through our spiritual leaders, we are being trained in Christ-likeness, and in our example of humility we become like Him.

Do you love correction? Learn to love it! If you want to experience personal revival, ask God and those in spiritual authority over you to give you correction. The more you learn to receive correction from others, the more easily you can receive direction from God's Spirit as He speaks in your heart.

Truth Can Come Through Anyone

If we want to learn how to receive and give spiritual correction, we must learn this simple fact: *All truth comes from God.* I bring this up because some of us say, "I am willing to receive correction and direction," but the truth is, we are willing to receive only if it comes from people we already respect. We pick and choose the people with whom we have no problem, and who have no issues with us. *Of course* we can receive their guidance—they talk and think just like us!

God's truth challenges. It must challenge us, because there is much in us that needs challenging, or it is probably not the full truth we need to hear. For this reason, I believe, God chooses people who are not like us, or who feel like grit on our skin, to bring His truth to us, for when we're challenged our real issues come out.

Many Christians love teaching. In parts of the Church today we love to run to seminars, conferences, and retreats. We buy the latest tapes. We listen to teaching series on the radio and from the pulpit. But we are not often directed or corrected by teaching per se. Teaching may tell us what to think, and even what to do, but hearing is not the same as doing. We mistakenly believe that knowing what is right is the same as doing it, but until that teaching becomes experience in our life, we are still babies, and it is the challenge of the spiritual parent that presses us to act on what we know.

The apostle Paul wrote to the churches in Corinth as a father bringing correction for their change. He said, "I write not these things to shame you, but as my beloved sons I warn you. For though ye have ten thousand instructors in Christ, yet have ye not many fathers: for in Christ Jesus I have begotten you through the gospel" (1 Corinthians 4:14–16, KJV).

Are you willing to submit to correction from spiritual "fathers"—meaning those in authority over you—whoever they may be? All truth comes from God. A man can receive God's truth from a woman, and an adult can receive truth from a child. A husband must be willing to hear correction from his wife, and vice versa. We ought not to cut our spouses short because their words sting with the truth. To do that is to give in to our pride.

The prophet Habakkuk said, "I . . . will watch to see what [God] will say unto me, and what I shall answer when I am reproved" (Habakkuk 2:1). This is the attitude we need when others correct us. God looks at our attitude to see if we are open to correction and direction. When He sees that our hearts are open and pliable, then He knows we are ready for His use.

Becoming a Spiritual Parent

You may never have heard God call you to be a spiritual parent, but if you are born again and you are following the leading of God, you *will* bear spiritual children. Being a parent, whether spiritual or natural, is a tremendous privilege, and also a great responsibility. For this reason, God will only use as spiritual parents those who are fully surrendered to Him. If you claim to be a spiritual authority of any kind, you can be certain that God will intervene in your life if He sees that you are getting off course or into sin, because others' lives will be affected in addition to yours. Beware: if you are in spiritual leadership and become a snake, lying and deceiving to protect your hidden sin, God will have to protect others from you. He will bring judgment on you—if not immediately, then certainly on that Great Day. James wrote, "My brethren, let not many of you become teachers, knowing that we shall receive a stricter judgment" (James 3:1). I am reminding you of this truth, whether you are a spiritual parent in the Church or in the home.

There is a goal to our training in Christ-likeness. It is to have our hearts so open to the directives of God, like Jesus, that we can become the spiritual parent to someone else. For in some measure we adults are accountable for the spiritual growth of others in our household (Ephesians 6:4; Deuteronomy 6:7). Our families should grow in wisdom because of the way we seek God for wisdom on their behalf. Husbands in particular are the heads of the house, as Christ is the head of the Church (Ephesians 5:22–33). I don't want to pass down my mistakes and weaknesses to either my spiritual or natural children. In the end, we will see ourselves show up in them. I would much prefer to pass along Christ-like traits rather than those of a snake, wouldn't you?

Now, I've been speaking about spiritual parenting, but you don't have to be thirty, forty, or fifty to become a reliable spiritual leader in the nature and character of Christ. In the churches under my care, we have seen young men of college age who have proven themselves to be spiritual fathers, and we have sent them out to pastor. The chapters of the college campus ministries we've founded are always led by students. We have even seen young people of fifteen or sixteen and children who are nine or ten who have a burden for fellow students and want to take over their school for Christ. They see the whole school as theirs. Imagine a young person of that age leading his classmates into Christ-likeness. Why not? Some kid is going to lead. Should we let a gang leader lead them? No. We need to train and encourage the young to lead. They can become spiritual fathers and mothers to other young people, leading the way in character growth.

Seeing as God Sees

Perhaps the trait that most helps us to become a spiritual mother or father is to see people as God sees them. In order to do this, we must consecrate our vision to God, saying, "Help me to see this person as you see them, not in any other way. Help me to lay aside prejudices and judgments. And help me to see myself as a role model."

What I am saying is that you must be willing to sacrifice all the ways you view people that are not the way He sees them. This always requires new dependence and constant sacrifice, because the way God works upon people is entirely opposite from the way we in our flesh see them (see 2 Corinthians 5:16). I can tell you this: If you don't have a heart for people of another race or culture or socioeconomic level, then your heart is *not* in agreement with God's heart. He is no respecter of persons (Romans 2:11). When we believe someone is beyond hope or is of lesser value, we have to pray, "God, change my heart for these people. Let me see them as valuable and worth giving my time and my energies for."

I have a vision for the inner cities of America. I believe it will require humility to go into the ruined neighborhoods where despair and violence reign and to father a new spirit in those who live there. I also believe that the principles of surrender that are required to do so are the same ones required wherever you are called to parent people in Christ. They are as follows:

- SEE that there is a harvest of lost people who are looking for God. He tells us, "The harvest is plentiful, but the workers are few. Ask the Lord of the harvest, therefore, to send out workers into his harvest field" (Luke 10:2, NIV).

- PRAY for people. Prayer gives us God's heart and mind toward others, in replacement of our own (see Romans 10:1–4).

- GO and WIN the lost and wandering. " 'Therefore go into the highways, and as many as you find, invite to the wedding.' So those servants went out into the highways and gathered together all whom they found, both bad and good. And the wedding hall was filled with guests" (Matthew 22:9–10). How do we win them?

- SPEAK DESTINY into the hearts of the people. Regardless of the outward circumstances or their sin, keep your faith alive. Tell them the good news of the Gospel. Tell them you are praying for them, that God has a hope and a future for them. " 'For I know the plans I have for you,' declares the Lord, 'plans to prosper you and not to harm you, plans to give you a hope and a future' " (Jeremiah 29:11, NIV).

- ◆ TRAIN the new converts. Take them to church, where they can be discipled by spiritual fathers. Set up neighborhood Bible studies, and have people come into your home to discuss godly principles for living; listen to their hurts and struggles; offer them peace through prayer.
- ◆ SEND them out as pastors and missionaries to the world. Once they are converted, teach them to surrender their lives to God so that through them He may reach and touch others.

No More Orphans

Toward the end of His time on earth, Jesus helped to prepare His disciples for the end of His earthly ministry with them. He had been with them for three years, teaching, guiding, correcting. Would they now be left alone?

"I shall not leave you as orphans," Jesus said, comforting them. "I shall come to you" (John 14:18, Berkeley). We typically do not think of Jesus in the role of a parent, but that is what He was—a living, breathing representation of the Father (John 14:9). And as every parent soon realizes, their job does not last forever. The real goal is to work ourselves out of a job, so that when our children leave the nest, they do not leave as "orphans," but as those able to become parents themselves.

Spiritual parenting is not a prescription to extract life-long dependence on a particular leader. It is our challenge to prepare leaders for the next generation.

To do this, we must be willing to walk with them through the fire.

chapter five

purified to
serve

"I always do those things that please Him." —JOHN 8:29

S OME YEARS AGO there was a song entitled
"Everybody's Dressing Up Jesus." It conveyed the
idea that sometimes we like to pick one aspect of
Jesus' identity or His work—especially a part we really
like—and act as if that one aspect is the most important
part. In the 1960s, for instance, Central American revolu-
tionaries depicted Jesus as a political radical because He
had presented an alternative to the religious institutions
of His day. In the Church, we may emphasize "Jesus, the
moral teacher," or "Jesus, the miracle worker." When we
choose only one aspect of the real Jesus to stand for the

whole, true person, we make a caricature of Jesus. Not surprisingly, this lesser Jesus looks oddly like us, because invariably we choose to exalt the side of Him that meets our needs, the part of Him we like. And so, once again, self-exaltation creeps in. This time it invades our attitudes toward God. We wind up saying to God, in attitude if not in words, "This is the way I see you, and therefore this is the way I'll serve you, because it's what I'm most comfortable doing."

If we are going to be real Christians in our service to God, then we need to approach our servitude to God in the same spirit of humility that Jesus demonstrated, and we need to take upon us the calling that He had, not a calling that we choose for ourselves. We will have to go through God's fire and be purified before we receive the zeal we need to carry out Jesus' calling on our lives.

Jesus' Calling

Jesus described His calling in this way:

> The Spirit of the Lord is upon me, because he hath anointed me to preach the gospel to the poor; he hath sent me to heal the brokenhearted, to preach deliverance to the captives, and recovering of sight to the

blind, to set at liberty them that are bruised—LUKE 4:18, KJV.

Jesus did not speak of His political agenda or His environmental or sociological agenda. He spoke of a higher goal: delivering people from those things that prevented them from entering into all that God had created them to be.

If we want to become able to liberate people into their destiny, as Jesus did, we will have to become more like Jesus. Like obedient children, we will have to learn how to watch what our Father does and then do what He does, because we know that it will please Him. Jesus said, "I do nothing of Myself; but as My Father taught Me, I speak these things. And He who sent Me is with Me. The Father has not left Me alone, for I always do those things that please Him" (John 8:28–29).

Jesus liberates people from the brokenheartedness of a godless, meaningless, sinful life of self-occupation. He frees people from spiritual blindness and the view that God is not actively, lovingly involved in their lives. He delivers those who are bruised by life and held captive to pains and failures, both past and present. He releases them from a life limited by temporary circumstances into an eternal view of reality.

When Jesus delivers people, His primary focus is not

freeing them from temporary trials and circumstances, because God can use all of our trials to change us into people who are more like Him. Although Christians historically have been driven to remedy natural problems, such as slavery, natural deliverance must not become our focus, or we will remain man-focused instead of God-focused. The ultimate goal of God is to change you in your innermost being, so that you can endure any natural circumstance and still remain like Him.

When you have been delivered by God, you are strong enough to face any circumstance because you have the inner peace and confidence that comes from learning to rest in God. Circumstances can change, sometimes radically, sometimes overnight. Jesus came to bring about a quiet revolution within you, whereby spiritual power slowly and quietly carries you through.

How does that inner change come about? It happens in many ways.

Underground

I would like to focus a bit on the work of underground movements. We can learn a lot from them about how God works in us and how we work alongside Him to deliver captives. The word "underground" has been used historically in a number of contexts to describe a revolutionary work that goes on secretly beneath the surface of society. For example, in the United States in the 1800s, an estimated 60,000 to 100,000 slaves escaped from the South along the path to freedom that was called the Underground Railroad. This was a network of hiding places and secret means of transport that took slaves into free territories in the Midwest and the North. The French Underground functioned during World War II, when Charles de Gaulle, the future president of France, led a movement from his exile in England to overthrow the Germans, who were occupying his homeland. Underground newspapers launch new, radical ideas before they are accepted by the general public. In underground movements, secrecy is always the key to success.

In the same way, Christians are successful in overthrowing evil in the world according to the level of their secret life in God. They will succeed if they are willing to work when no one else is around, when no one sees them, when no one applauds what they do. The word "underground" implies something done in secret. Jesus worked in the open, of course, as He delivered people with His teaching and His miracles. But He also worked in secret, sometimes forbidding His followers to make known who He really was—the Son of God.

Here is the first clue about working alongside with God: We do not trumpet or boast about what we are doing. The devil is full of pride, and when we prefer the limelight to the secret service of God, we need to examine ourselves and the source of our actions. Much of what the Church does is on public display, such as Sunday worship services, and this is necessary, but public displays are not the Church's true source of strength. The size of the building or the number of people in the congregation do not determine its influence. A church can have thousands coming on Sunday but hardly anybody willing to become like Jesus.

Jesus dealt mostly with the strength that comes through the secret life of the heart. As Christians we will be successful in overthrowing evil only as we grow strong in our secret life in God. And so I ask: How well developed is your secret prayer life? Do you fast in secret? Do you give secretly, so that no one can give you the credit? Do you serve in secret, so that others are blessed without knowing you were the source of God's goodness to them?

Getting the Word Out

In any movement that has influence—even ungodly movements—you will find people who have surrendered themselves, subordinating their lives to a greater purpose. They lay down everything for "the cause," to spread the word that defines the movement and calls people together to do its work. In the early nineteenth century, Christians involved in the abolition of slavery began their efforts to get the word out. They published tracts and books. But mostly, they went out into their own neighborhoods and explained the principles of the Bible that related to their cause. They saw themselves as spiritual fathers and mothers of their neighborhoods, and they were determined to bring the will and work of heaven down to earth.

A few years ago the mayor of Dayton, Ohio, asked me what advice I would give him as a man of God. I said he should govern by godly convictions and be willing to be a one-term mayor. In this way, he would pioneer a new standard and take away any political agendas he might have had related to his next term. He did that, and also won a second term as mayor.

We have to get back to declaring the Word for God, not only on Sunday morning but also in our neighborhoods and at our jobs. We need to see ourselves as those who are asked by God to join with Him in bringing words of deliverance to our neighborhoods, cities, and nations. We should not be ashamed to ask our leaders as well as our neighbors, "Where do you stand with God? Do you know

Him?" We cannot be ashamed of God, embarrassed to introduce others to Him personally *and* work in His causes. We need to declare His name by giving Him honor, and we need to do so with our godly lives as well as with our mouths. If our walk does not match our talk, people will not listen to our words.

When I first became a pastor, I didn't think about the Church and its work with God in deliverance. I didn't see myself and other Christians as deliverers. I was thinking about what people would expect on Sunday morning. Every week I would plan the service, oversee the choir, make sure we had enough ushers and that the place was clean, and work hard on a nice sermon. Those seem like logical things for a pastor to do, but I was missing the true heart of pastoring. I was leading people into religion, which involves all of the externals of church activities, but I wasn't leading them into a relationship with the living God so that God could change them and use them to reach this generation. Because I was religious, I was producing Christian people who were religious, not Christians shaped in the humble, God-serving spirit of Jesus Christ.

Religious people are often nice, but sometimes they are superficial. They have no depth of spirit. They talk one way when they are in a church service and another way when they get to their jobs. They sing songs on Sunday morning, and they say "Praise God" and "Bless the Lord" to one another. But after they move outside the doors they are too proud to use the same language in the rest of the world. *After all*, they wonder, *what would other people think?*

The question is not whether we talk like Christians. It is whether or not we are willing to live and do the work of Christians in the world. Jesus wants us to live with a sense of His humility, taking His life and His work upon us, because everywhere we go we'll find captives needing some aspect of God's release. Then, if our lifestyle comes from God and God approves our life, people in the world won't mind hearing us say "Praise God." They will begin to say "Praise God" with us, because when they have a need they see that we have more than religion to offer them. They see we are in touch with a real God who sets real people free and makes them really genuine.

When I woke up to this characteristic of Jesus—His genuineness—I saw the difference between my religious spirit and God's Holy Spirit. Jesus was the same in the synagogue—with the Pharisees, scribes, and Sadducees—as He was walking on the street among sinners. He was not one way with religious people, another way with common people. The disciples who followed Him didn't see a dichotomy in His life. There was no hypocrisy, no contradictions, and no shadows. Jesus could deliver people from bondage because He was not bound by any secret sin. He had no darkness inside of Him, so He could bring people into the light. Our lack of genuineness—our lies, deceptions, and lack of integrity—binds us in secretiveness and darkness, but openness can set us free. When I saw the difference between religious acts and a life that was lived openly, honestly, in the light with God, I saw a life of deadness and conformity to tradition versus a life of authenticity and real spiritual strength. I decided that I no longer wanted religion. I wanted reality. I wanted to follow God. And I have been on that road ever since.

Do you want to follow God? Do you want to be able to release people with His words? If so, you must be willing to take on the challenge of becoming not just a follower of God but also a spiritual leader of others. When we become His followers, taking on His mission, we will also become leaders. "Followership" to leadership. That is the pattern.

Two People Called Moses

We can learn something about humility in leadership from two different people known as Moses.

In the Bible, Moses was a deliverer who gave glory to God. He wasn't flashy. He wasn't playing for the crowd. He was leading millions of people across the desert, with a giant pillar of cloud before him, but inside he had learned to stay low. The Bible says that Moses was "very meek" (Numbers 12:3, KJV). He didn't start out meek. When he was younger, he had murdered an Egyptian who was beating an Israeli slave, and he had to run for his life. However, God had trained him on the backside of the mountain to control his emotions and his zeal.

Moses had to learn not to defend himself, because God was his Defender. When you know you are called to greatness, it's hard to stay low and not strike back against people who challenge your authority, especially those who are close to you. Moses faced dissent and humiliation from his own brother and sister, Aaron and Miriam. They claimed that Moses had disqualified himself as the leader of Israel because he had chosen for his wife a black Ethiopian (Numbers 12:1–15). They said, "Has the LORD indeed spoken only through Moses? Has He not spoken through us also?" (Numbers 12:2). They were exalting themselves, as the devil had done. They were looking at external qualifications, "but the LORD looks at the heart" (1 Samuel 16:7). They didn't consider his relationship with God a proper qualification for leadership.

When Aaron and Miriam challenged Moses' credentials as a deliverer, he didn't defend himself. He waited and let God defend him, and God's wrath was much more severe than anything that he could have done. The Bible says that when Aaron and Miriam spoke, "the LORD heard it" (Numbers 12:2, KJV). The thought that the Lord hears us should put the fear of God on us. Our words against our leaders are being judged in heaven. When you speak against God's leaders, His wrath is real.

God called Moses His friend, and He defended His friend against the attacks to his leadership by striking Miriam with leprosy. Moses did not have one ounce of revenge in him. When he saw God's judgment against his sister, he cried out to the Lord, "Please heal her, O God, I pray!" (Numbers 12:13). That is a mark of greatness. One of the most important steps you can take as you move into your calling is to surrender your pride and become humble. Constantly examine your secret motives to see if your heart is right. As your influence increases, learn to trust God to establish your authority. Don't try to establish your authority by your own efforts. When you are called to be a deliverer, you are agreeing to be a man or woman who is a living demonstration of forgiveness and love for we are leading people in spirit toward a promised land where there is reconciliation with God himself.

The second "Moses" from whom we can learn about humility in leadership is Harriet Tubman. As a child, Harriet was a slave who was continually beaten for her willfulness. Somehow, through the divine hand of God, Harriet came to know Christ. Suddenly her outward fight became a lifetime battle to stay inwardly surrendered to God—so that her energies would not be wasted on misdirecting or misusing her anger. Her whole spirit changed. As she herself said, "I prayed to God to make me strong and able to fight and that's what I've allers prayed for ever since."[7]

Harriet's first fight was against her own unbelief and doubt. She did not see herself as qualified to be a deliverer. She was poor and illiterate. She had received permanent brain damage from a blow to the head that occurred when her master threw a heavy weight at another slave, and accidentally hit her instead. But God's call to Harriet persisted, and she learned that we can never use weakness as an excuse. Our call in the work of delivering this world is a call to rely on Christ.

A major turning point in Harriet's life came when she was still a slave. It was a time of trial when God developed the quality of meekness in her. She lay sick in bed for several months, and all the time her master kept trying to sell her, constantly bringing a parade of buyers to look at her. This is how her biographer, Sarah Bradford, quoted Harriet's account of those events.

As I lay so sick on my bed, from Christmas till March, I was always praying for poor ole master. 'Pears like I didn't do nothing but pray for ole master. "Oh, Lord, convert ole master; Oh, dear Lord, change dat man's heart, and make him a Christian." And all the time he was bringing men to look at me, and dey stood there saying what dey would give, and what dey would take, and al I could say was, "Oh, Lord, convert ole master." Den I heard dat as soon as I was able to move I was to be sent with my brudders, in the chain-gang to de far South. Then I changed my prayer, and I said, "Lord, if you ain't never going to change dat man's heart, kill him, Lord, and take him out of de way, so he won't do no more mischief." Next ting I heard ole master was dead; and he died just as he lived, a wicked, bad man. Oh, den it 'peared like I would give de world full of silver and gold, if I had, to bring dat pore soul back. I would give myself; I would give eberyting! But he was gone, I couldn't pray for him no more.[8]

Tremendous conviction came to Harriet's heart after her slave master died. The intensity of our relationship with God increases with each new conviction. Harriet didn't have religion. She had a relationship with a real God. She had the internal strength to pray for the salvation of the man who was trying to sell her, and then she repented when he died.

You can't offer God a couple of hours on Sunday and call

yourself a serious Christian. It's like getting a pep pill—or a "gos-pill"—and then going out and living like the devil. If God is real, you want the Lord to show up in your own life at the level He showed up in Harriet Tubman's life. You want to constantly give yourself over to Him. The proof of your dedication is not what you do at a Sunday service, but what you do and how you live in the world where there is darkness.

Let your light shine in the darkness by letting Him fill you with His light. Don't make people have to look for God in your life, but make His presence so real that they can find Him in you because you are letting Him break through like the sun on a dark day. When it is dark out in the world, that is when the light that is in you shines brightest.

In 1849, when she was almost thirty years old, Harriet escaped from a plantation on the eastern shore of Maryland. Through great trials she made her way north by the Underground Railroad. The next year, she slipped boldly back into Maryland to rescue members of her family. She returned again and again to bring people out of suffering and bondage. When she discovered that her husband had remarried and would not even see her, she made an even greater resolve to be wed to the calling that God had placed in her heart.

Seven or eight times Harriet returned to the neighborhood of her former home. She was always at the risk of death in the most terrible forms. Each time, she brought away a company of fugitive slaves, and led them safely to the free States, or to Canada. Over time, she escorted some three hundred slaves to freedom. It was no wonder that among the slaves she was known best by the name "Moses, the deliverer." Neither the Moses of the Bible nor Harriet Tubman had superficial religion. They had a real relationship with the real God. Some Christians say they "got religion" in a positive sense, but all they may really be doing is putting on Adam's wilted and dying fig leaves (Genesis 3). They are covering up and looking good in their own eyes, but God sees their sin.

If we want the Lord to involve us in His work of delivering the world from its suffering and slavery we, too, must give ourselves over to Him in humble service. The proof of our dedication is not what we do on Sunday morning. It is what we do and how we carry His light into the world, where the darkness is.

Consecration

People are looking for the light of God that will lead them out of their confusion, hurt, and darkness. We, as followers of Christ, are called to be that light—light that leads. Jesus said of us, "You are the light of the world" (Matthew 5:14). But light shines best through something that is clean and clear. When a window is dirty, what shines through is only a dim, smudgy version of the light that could pass through. Every one of us Christians is called to let Jesus shine through us. In humility, we are called to consecrate ourselves—that is, to clean up our lives and set aside our own agendas in order to do God's work of delivering people.

At the foundation of our commitment to follow God is the act of consecration. This is not a one-time event. It is an ongoing action of turning ourselves over to God to be cleansed of selfish motives and every type of sinful action. The Bible says, "Having therefore these promises, dearly beloved, let us cleanse ourselves from all filthiness of the flesh and spirit, perfecting holiness in the fear of God" (2 Corinthians 7:1, KJV). God trains us to become purified through the process of consecration, by which we are cleansed so that the light of God shines through.

We need to commit ourselves earnestly to God, asking Him to give us the gift of devotion—the willingness to go with God wherever He wants us to go. To let go of all self-seeking motives, and work "in secret" without recognition. To declare the Word of God in our words and deeds. To be clean from within so God's light can shine in us, and through us to others.

As we let go of our lives and follow the direction of God,

as Moses and Harriet Tubman did, we are walking in the humility of Christ Jesus. Then we know we are not trying to work in our own power. Rather, we are relying on a power far more vast than our own to bring healing, salvation, and deliverance to the world.

Following the Fire

God sent Moses to lead the people of Israel out of their bondage in Egypt into the promised land, but sometimes the people couldn't see it. They didn't want to move forward. All they could see were the obstacles.

When we are in bondage to sin, or guilt, or fear, it immobilizes us. It prevents us from doing the work of God. To become free, we cannot stay where we are. We have to move out of our complacency or frustration. This will not usually be comfortable. Change almost always seems to involve an element of risk and tension. It is interesting that after all was said and done, only those Israelites who were twenty and under when they left Egypt eventually made it into the promised land. The older we are, the less change seems palatable. But it is necessary for us to move on in the work God has called us to do.

All in all, one or two million Israelites walked with Moses out of their captivity in Egypt, across the Red Sea, and into the desert. Talk about change! From a lush river valley to the barren wilderness. Yet this was their path to freedom. In order to guide them, God sent a cloud by day and a pillar of fire by night. Fire provided light and warmth. It was a comfort and encouragement, particularly on a chilly night in the desert. But the fire was also a reminder of what God was doing in their lives: purifying them like gold, making them ready for the promised land, tempering their resolve for the battles ahead.

If we are to be changed into the people God would have us be, we too must follow the fire. We can only be free from our bondage if we allow God to lead us out of it. He has made a way through Jesus, the Living Word of God. As we keep our eyes on Him, "the author and finisher of our faith" (Hebrews 12:2), we will receive courage and confidence to allow God to purify us in the fire, to make us into the kind of servants He can use.

We have been playing church. Now we must become the Church. It should be said of us that we not only care about our own freedom, but that we are also willing to be changed and sacrifice our own desires in order to set others free. Deliverance happens one person at a time, but it does not happen in isolation. True deliverance happens in the context of the body of Christ. We need each other and the gifts Christ has given to us. Only in unity can we walk out God's vision for deliverance—both for ourselves and for those around us.

chapter six

humility— the foundation of unity

". . . till we all come to the unity of the faith and of the
knowledge of the Son of God, to a perfect man, to the
measure of the stature of the fullness of Christ."

—EPHESIANS 4:13

I N MATTHEW'S GOSPEL, Jesus gave us an astonish-
ing promise: "Blessed are the meek, for they shall inherit the earth" (Matthew 5:5). "Meek" is, of course,
another word for "humble." Many of us read that and
think, *Wonderful. The earth will be ours. We will rule with God
one day over a new earth* (see Revelation 21:1). And so we
will. But first we must remember that God cannot use us to
carry out His will on earth if we hold on to a spirit that rises
up against Him and strikes out on its own. That old snake
inside of us dies very hard. And so God must train us in the
lowly spirit of Christ, so that we love to do His will and not

our own. God is not going to turn the world over to the Church to run on our own—not later, and most definitely not now. First, He must make us meek.

In order for Christians to inherit the earth, I believe that we will have to become unified. And in order to become unified we will have to become humble and broken. When Jesus took the bread at the Last Supper, He blessed the bread and broke it. A lot of what we are going through in our struggles within the body of Christ centers around our unwillingness to be humbled. We all want to be independent, strong in ourselves, *not* interdependent. God insists that we who call ourselves members of the body of Christ become like Christ. That is how He blesses us. He is not going to let us go until we enter into that blessing of unity through humility.

John Wesley on Unity

John Wesley was the founder of the Methodist Church. God used him to bring a great revival, both in England and in America. But before he was greatly used of God, Wesley had to go through God's training, which made him meek.

First, he made the discovery that although he had been leading a so-called "Holy Club" at Oxford University and had even been a missionary to the colony of Georgia, he was not saved. Then, after Wesley was awakened to faith in Jesus Christ, he was labeled as "controversial" by other Christians. Branded. He didn't leave the Church of England, but many of those pastors would not allow him to preach in their churches. They rejected him. Not only that, but his friend from the "Holy Club," George Whitefield, whom God was using in America's great spiritual awakening, disagreed with Wesley on points of doctrine. Even Whitefield distanced himself, causing Wesley more suffering. Despite all of these challenges, and all of this personal breaking, Wesley never lost the desire that God had given him to see the body of Christ come into unity. He understood that in order for us to come to unity, to again become God's people who are ready to rule with Him, we must be broken.

Here is an excerpt on unity from one of his messages on the fruits of a living faith—the Church becoming one family together.

By these marks, by these fruits of a living faith, do we labour to distinguish ourselves from the unbelieving world from all those whose minds or lives are not according to the Gospel of Christ. But from real Christians, of whatsoever denomination they be, we earnestly desire not to be distinguished at all, not from any who sincerely follow after what they know they have not yet attained.[9]

Wesley was willing to be meek. He did not lash out at those who rejected and insulted him. He kept God's greater vision in mind.

Meekness is strength under control. It is the quality that makes us directable under God. It also keeps us from having a spirit that rises up above our brothers and sisters to lord it over them, judge them, or use them for our own ends. We cannot fulfill God's will to reach people if we abuse them. Meekness puts us at the level of "other" people—even makes us willing to go lower than others, to be servant-leaders in the spirit of Christ. Meekness is what keeps us growing together into unity, as a whole body of believers God can use together. This is His plan: to create a people who are one in Him.

In order for Christians to inherit the earth, we must allow God to work in us to make us unified. And in order to become unified we first have to be broken—the way wild, maverick stallions have to be made docile in the hands of a trainer.

Our Example

Have you met anybody meek lately in the church? Usually they're the old mothers who have raised several generations of children on fifty cents a day, or the kindly white-haired missionaries who have been in the trenches with the lost. They've been fighting the battle for souls—first for their own souls, or those in their families, or else for the souls of multitudes in forgotten places. Too often we overlook these meek ones. We don't even recognize them as the spiritual giants they are. God does. We focus on the flashy, "upfront" people, and call them leaders. It's time to recognize that they may have power on earth; but does their power come from God or from their own personality? From the Holy Spirit or their ability to implement marketing principles?

The powerful and the flashy are not always the best example, unless underneath it all they are humble servants of God. The best example to follow is Jesus. When Jesus took the bread at the Last Supper, He blessed it, and broke it, and then He said, "Take, eat: this is my body, which is broken for you: this do in remembrance of me" (1 Corinthians 11:24, KJV). As the body of Christ, we are blessed—but then we, too, must be broken. God has to subject us to breaking because of our independence and stubbornness. He is not going to let us go until we enter into that blessing of unity through brokenness. Brokenness is the lasting wealth of the Christian. It is the ability to allow circumstances, situations, or hardships to be remedied by Christ only—not to take one step outside of the character of Christ. In this, Christ is our example.

When He gave His disciples the bread at the Last Supper, Jesus said, "This is My body which is given for you; do this in *remembrance of me*" (Luke 22:19, italics added by author). We must solemnly realize, every time we eat the bread and drink the cup, that we are pledging ourselves to re-enact in our very lives the death of the One who is our example. We are told to go back to this meal again and again until the Master returns. We are to meditate on it—to "chew on" its meaning, so that we come to really understand what we are being asked to do. We are to live every day with a sense of humility and brokenness before God, so that we can live in communion with Him and with one another.

Many Christian traditions use the word Eucharist for the communion service. That is the first century Greek word for this celebration, and it means to be grateful for favor shown. It is a reminder of God's great gift of Jesus' death on the cross—the one true sacrifice for our sins. It also recalls the gift of His resurrection. After three days He got up and opened heaven so that now we have access to the Father.

The word "communion" is also a translation of the Greek word *koinonia*, which means "fellowship." This gift of fellowship allows us to come to God freely, every day, and to become one with Him and with one another (see John 17:21). A key to our fellowship is learning how to identify with Jesus, the lowly, in both His death and His resurrection. The Apostle Paul tells us that if we are "unified with him like this in his death, we will certainly also be unified with him in his resurrection" (Romans 6:5, NIV).

What does it mean to be unified with Christ in His death? It means that we recognize in ourselves all the old ways of the snake that are in us, all the things that we do that rise up against God, and against our brothers and sisters. The psalmist said, "Search me, O God, and know my heart: try me, and know my thoughts: And see if there be any wicked way in me, and lead me in the way everlasting" (Psalms 139:23–24, KJV). Real communion every day with the Father requires us to examine ourselves to see if there is an unsurrendered will in us. Then God can clean us and deliver us.

We cannot help deliver others to God if we ourselves have not experienced His inner brokenness and have come to walk in His life. As we allow God to show us the truth about ourselves, we can recognize the old self-will that needs to be put aside and left to die. We go down with Him in humility so that we can go up to the Father in prayer. It is not enough to bend the will in prayer. We must die fully to the self-will. "For ye are dead, and your life is hid with Christ in God" (Colossians 3:3, KJV).

"We were therefore buried with him through baptism into death in order that, just as Christ was raised from the dead through the glory of the Father, we too may live a new life" (Romans 6:4 NIV). Jesus was raised from death to sit at the right hand of God, where He now rules. Our place is to rule and reign with Him, resting in the authority of God, who created us for *His* purposes, not ours. As Augustine said in his *Confessions* many centuries ago, "[T]hou hast made us for thyself and restless is our heart until it comes to rest in thee."[10]

Fellowship of the Spirit

You may be reading along as I speak about humility and brokenness and resting in God and not think too much about it—until you have to apply it in your own life, such as in your relationship with the people in your own home.

I remember one Sunday when I arrived at church and

began preparing to preach, but I was so guilt-ridden about a disagreement with my wife that morning that I had to call her on the phone at home. I didn't have time to tell my assistant to leave the room, so I just blurted it out in front of her. I said, "Honey, when I read the Scriptures I knew I had to call you and say, 'Would you forgive me?' " She did.

That morning when I was talking to her, I saw that I was not as serious a Christian as I thought I was. I needed to be more careful in my relationship with my wife. When I start defending myself to her, that just proves that there are unbroken areas in me. It is so tempting to fight back when someone tells us something that we don't want to hear, but we have to resist. We have to be strong for their sakes, and for the sake of unity in the home and in the body of Christ.

Disharmony is rooted in pride. It misrepresents God. There is harmony in heaven, so there must be harmony in our relationships on earth. When we die to self and live a resurrected life, something changes inside of us. The spirit of the lowly One is seen in us. We are "raised" to a new life under God's authority, and then we are authentic. Genuine. People are turned off from Christianity when we are not genuine—when we talk principles but don't live by them. For instance, we say Christianity is based on love but then we rise up and strike back and do not love one another in the Church. Or we look down on people who belong to a different denomination than we do. Outsiders are turned off, because they see that we are not committed in reality to the love we *say* we are committed to. They do not see in us the life of Jesus, Who demonstrated the very principle of love—which is to lay down your life for another. If they hear lowliness but they see the snake—our inconsistency speaks more loudly than our words. We are not fooling anyone. If, however, we say we are in communion with God, then the Spirit of Christ will be evident in our lives. We will be cleansed of the desire to be part of party factions with their roots of pride, and unity will come as a result.

My unity with my wife has overflowed in the unity of my leaders with their wives. Almost all of the pastors and leaders who have come from the spiritual children we have raised over the years have stayed married and grown more and more in love with one another. Meekness is not weakness. It is a strong fiber that holds together the cords of matrimony, as well as the Church.

Personally, I believe God wants to pour out on this world a tidal wave of glory. That will be seen in the light generated when the Church, Christ's body, comes together as one. First, we have to be humbled by a deeper realization—that we *cannot* do what the Bible says and love one another until we learn meekness, and we will not be able to develop in meekness without the Spirit of Christ, the Holy Spirit. And so, before the wave of glory, there will be times of self-examination and sadness. We will see our failures and turn to the Lord and receive from Him the ability to love others as we love ourselves. We will die to ourselves as we abandon ourselves to Him. That is why we must continually be receiving the life of the Lord, which our Lord's Supper represents. Unless we receive a new spirit in us we are incapable of doing the greater work of God. But as we lower ourselves, the Father pours out the Holy Spirit, who came at Pentecost, to flow through us like a river of living water. Each time we do this we have a stronger understanding of what we need, which always includes more humility—more surrender to the God who seeks to make us one in love.

The prophet Ezekiel wrote, "Then I will give them one heart, and I will put a new spirit within them, and take the stony heart out of their flesh, and give them a heart of flesh, that they may walk in My statutes and keep My judgments and do them; and they shall be My people, and I will be their God" (Ezekiel 11:19–20).

Jesus humbled Himself and came to the earth so that we might have access to the Father's heart. He opened the way for the Spirit to be poured out so that our communion with God might be real, vital.

The Apostle Paul clearly understood the need to commune with God in Spirit, to identify with His death so that we might be raised to a new kind of life. He also understood the profound mystery of God revealed through a unified body here on earth. Paul referred to himself as the least apostle, but he did not start out with that humble attitude. Not by far. He was a proud scholar who thought he knew everything until God broke through to him. He thought he had righteousness in him until he was crushed and pride was revealed. He became a great unifier of the Church, but he started out as a destroyer (see Galatians 1:13).

He had never known Jesus as a man and therefore didn't have the relationship that the other apostles had as Jesus' disciples. Yet God used Paul to write about *seventy-five percent of the New Testament*. Once he embraced humility, he was not afraid to admit his frailties. In the midst of each challenge, he could hear God say, "My grace is sufficient for you" (2 Corinthians 12:9). It took a lot of training at the hands of God for Paul to recognize his need for grace.

Paul was raised a devout Pharisee, a "Hebrew of the Hebrews" (Philippians 3:5). He was taught by the best Jewish scholars, and knew every facet of the law. What he did not have was a genuine relationship with God. He could recite the Scriptures—but he needed to embrace the living God behind the Scriptures.

This is a problem many Christians have. They say they love God and love His Word, but when it comes to loving other Christians who do not hold to all the same doctrines or practices, they cut people off and distance themselves. They look down on people of another denomination. They don't want to associate with them. From heaven, divided Christians look like opposing teams on a basketball court, fighting for the same ball. They don't come together and say, "Teach me what you know and I'll share what I know. Tell me your concerns for the world, and I'll tell you mine." Instead, the people on one side, who think they know the Bible better than the people on the other side, forget to love one another, and let the superior attitude of a snake come in to keep them divided and weak. They are like Paul *before* his conversion.

Paul thought he was serving God when he looked down on the followers of Christ, seeing himself as superior. He consented to Stephen's death, making Stephen a martyr. Paul also went from house to house looking for believers so that he could persecute and imprison them. Of course we do not go to these extremes, but with our divisive pride we still oppress the body of Christ. Paul did not change his attitude until he had an undeniable encounter with the living God that knocked him—quite literally—off his high horse.

As he was on his way to Damascus to arrest and persecute the Christians, suddenly a light shone brightly around Paul. He fell to the ground and heard a voice from heaven. It was Jesus. Instead of arguing, Paul humbled himself and said, "Lord, what do You want me to do?" (see Acts 9). Paul was physically blind for three days after that experience— and it was during this time that he learned to see by faith. God revealed to Paul that not only was he harming people but also that he was fighting against God (Acts 9:5).

We need this revelation—all of us who call ourselves Christians. We will have doctrinal differences, and differences in practice, too, but I always try to let God be God. He uses a lot of people whom I would have disqualified. One example is the Southern Baptists. Some of my black brethren disqualify them on the basis of racism. The Southern Baptists had the character to repent a few years ago because they had founded their denomination on the basis of racism. Isn't it a wonder that over the past century—in spite of racism—that they have probably won more people to Christ than anyone else? When we only seek to pull apart from other Christians, when we secretly judge, criticize, and condemn them, we are working against God Himself, who works to make us one in Christ.

Paul regained his sight when a Christian by the name of Ananias prayed for him. Ananias himself had to overcome his judgmentalism before he would even go to see Paul. He argued with God, " 'Lord, I have heard from many about this man, how much harm he has done to Your saints in Jerusalem. And here he has authority from the chief priests to bind all who call on Your name.' But the Lord said to him, 'Go, for he is a chosen vessel of Mine to bear My name before Gentiles, kings, and the children of Israel. For I will show him how many things he must suffer for My name's sake' " (Acts 9:13–16).

Are you a Paul? Are you an Ananias? Are you like me when I was rising up in pride against my wife? Eventually, Paul became a great preacher of the Gospel of Jesus Christ. He could have been living the easy life as a Pharisee. Instead, he decided to follow after Jesus and suffer persecution. He was almost beaten to death, stoned, robbed. He went through it all for the sake of the Gospel. He laid everything aside to be a disciple of Christ. Wherever he went, he preached a message of God's grace.

Do we submit ourselves to other Christians, letting them see our need and weakness and lack? Do we trust that God hears their prayers? Or do we pridefully reject anything they might offer us because we deem them "not righteous"? If so, we will never move beyond our divisive spirit, nor let the Holy Spirit fill us. We will never be able to declare with real power the message "Christ is risen," because He will not have risen inside of us.

It is important to walk every day with a divine sense of communion, an understanding that you are walking with the Lord in His resurrection. You are clean today, because of what Jesus did on the cross. You are identifying with His death. Therefore, you are also identifying with His resurrection.

Pride of Grace

There is another way we destroy the spirit of unity in the body God wants to build. As we have been seeing, it is a common thing in the Christian community to compare ourselves with one another, to believe we are more favored than others. But that is wrong.

The apostle Paul wrote, "We dare not . . . compare ourselves with some that commend themselves: but they measuring themselves by themselves, and comparing themselves among themselves, are not wise" (2 Corinthians 10:12, KJV). The moment we begin to compare ourselves with other human beings, we are headed down the wrong road—the road to self-exaltation where we put ourselves up and other Christians down. Sadly, even church leaders wind up competing over who has the biggest mailing list, the most members, the most TV stations and the biggest budgets. Pastors pride themselves in having a "mega-church," secretly believing the size of their church is a measure of their own "righteousness." They don't realize that they have *their* place in the body of Christ by grace alone.

As mentioned earlier, John Wesley had a vision for unity among Christians that helped him to lead a spiritual awakening and build a movement while at the same time maintaining relationships with men like George Whitefield who disagreed with his theology. A key factor in Wesley's heart for reconciliation was what he was taught as a child by his godly mother, Susanna Wesley. Even after her children were grown, Susanna reminded them to remain humble, not just in public but also in that secret place of the heart. Here is an excerpt on humility from one of her letters to her son Samuel Wesley, Jr.:

[S]eriously consider your own many failings, which the world cannot take notice of because they were so private; and if still, upon comparison, you seem better than others are, then ask yourself who is it that makes you to differ, and let God have all the praise, since of ourselves we can do nothing. It is he that worketh in us both to will and to do of his own good pleasure, and if at any time you have vainly ascribed the glory of any good performance to yourself, humble yourself for it before God, and give him the glory of his grace for the future.¹¹

Humility begins with self-honesty. What about me is most valuable to God? We have to stop looking at externals such as the number of members or the size of the budget, and ask, "Am I becoming more like Christ?" We must stop "measuring ourselves by ourselves" and with our jealousies doing damage to the body of Christ. *God values His nature being reproduced in us more than any external accomplishment that we can boast about on our own.*

What I am saying is that sometimes we can become deceived by the blessings of God. We believe He has blessed us in our work, our church, our ministry because we were so right and deserving—not merely because we were chosen. Moses told the people of Israel,

> The LORD did not set His love on you nor choose you because you were more in number than any other people, for you were the least of all peoples; but because the LORD loves you, and because He would keep the oath which He swore to your fathers, the LORD has brought you out with a mighty hand, and redeemed you from the house of bondage, from the hand of Pharaoh king of Egypt. Therefore know that the LORD your God, He is

God, the faithful God who keeps covenant and mercy for a thousand generations with those who love Him and keep His commandments—Deuteronomy 7:7–9.

The worst thing that can happen to us is that we get self-deceived and think we are really something. When that happens we judge other people by what they have on the outside, while our world dies from a lack of substance within. God wants to teach us not to exalt ourselves and think we are somebody just because He is using us. He uses us in His work because He has mercy on whomever He wants to have mercy (see Exodus 33:19; Romans 9:15).

Do we see this clearly? The disciples of Jesus hoped for positions and power. They thought that He would set up an earthly kingdom and that they would be ruling next to Him. On one occasion the mother of James and John even requested a special position for her sons. She asked if they could sit on the left and on the right of Jesus in His kingdom (Matthew 20:20–28). Perhaps these sons of Zebedee were looking for some preferential treatment because they were a part of the "big three"—Jesus' inner-most circle. In their pride they presumed they had done something to earn them this position. They had "pride of grace."

What they failed to realize was that Jesus' kingdom is

not of this world, and that the way to rule with Him was through suffering on the earth.

> [W]hoever wishes to become great among you shall be your servant, and whoever wishes to be first among you shall be your slave; just as the Son of Man did not come to be served, but to serve, and to give His life a ransom for many—MATTHEW 20:26–28, NASB.

They were chosen all right. Chosen to suffer the rejections and pain Jesus himself was to suffer.

Recently I have read some disturbing articles in Christian publications about certain high-profile Christian pastors who are getting divorced and saying it is God's will. One man said that he had made a mistake and married the wrong woman, and so he divorced her and married someone else. That would have been bad enough, but the pastor who performed the ceremony with the new bride was also a well-known pastor with influence over thousands of people.

The Witness in Our Hearts

We cannot get around the fact that Jesus preached a message of humility and suffering. Sadly, many pastors today say that humility is too harsh a message for "the average

Christian," let alone general audiences. Could it be that they don't want to take the low road with Jesus themselves, and they also will preach whatever it takes to keep "the great multitudes" following them?

Instead of vying for position, at any level of the body of Christ, we must all learn what it means to follow Jesus. When we are stepped on we will strike back instead of using the power God gives us to bless and deliver those around us from evil and self-centeredness.

Today so many Christians—leaders and followers alike—are seeking God's power. Yet we will know that revival is about to come with His power when we can be reviled and not exact revenge. God wants to give us power to be humble servants, trusting Him to do what is just instead of demanding justice ourselves. We are to be just like His Son, Jesus, "who, when He was reviled, did not revile in return; when He suffered, He did not threaten, but committed Himself to Him who judges righteously" (1 Peter 2:23).

Therefore, being like Him, "Being reviled, we bless; being persecuted, we endure; being defamed, we entreat. We have been made as the filth of the world, the offscouring of all things until now" (1 Corinthians 4:12–13). This passage on the supernatural strength that God gives us in the face of humiliation is especially graphic in *The Message, The New Testament in Contemporary Language*, by Eugene H.

Peterson. "It seems to me that God has put us who bear his Message on stage in a theater in which no one wants to buy a ticket. We're something everyone stands around and stares at, like an accident in the street. We're the Messiah's misfits."

When we see who we are in relationship to who God is, then can we handle power and authority in a way that reveals God's glory and not our own.

Taking the Low Road

Throughout Christian history, many in the body have discovered the low road of humility. Christ has become more real to them. Their understanding of unconditional love and service has increased. Those who were in positions of authority did not strive for positions of honor, but considered themselves brothers and sisters who were going for Christ-likeness together with the rest of the saints.

One of these was C. H. Mason, mentioned earlier. At one point he became aware of an argument that two of his overseers were having over their territories in the Church of God in Christ. Each one felt the other had usurped some of his authority. These two men came to Bishop Mason to settle their disagreement, and yet this wise man did not try to give them any advice. He just asked them to get down on their knees with him and pray. For a few hours, he kept them on their knees. Eventually he asked them what they were hearing from God.

One said, "I really appreciated the prayer time, but we still need to know how we are going to solve this dispute."

The other agreed. "We need your judgment on this matter. We need an answer."

Mason took them back to prayer for a few more hours. Then he asked them again.

The men were very agitated, and so he took them back to prayer a third time.

After praying most of the day, Mason asked them what they were going to do. Both men blurted out at the same time, "Bishop Mason, he can have my territory!" Daddy Mason took them on a road they had seldom traveled—the road to humility. Their brokenness then became the foundation of a new unity through which God began to work in mighty ways in each of their jurisdictions.

Humility, The Foundation of Unity

The Bible says, "If the foundations be destroyed, what can the righteous do?" (Psalm 11:3, KJV). A foundational principle of the Church that has been almost destroyed is humility—the lowliness of Christ.

There are three things we can act upon, as we pray and ask God to build new unity in the body of Christ where we are.

* First of all, when a brother or sister is offended with us, we don't need to analyze the situation in a way that satisfies our pride. We need to go to the other person, repent, and seek peace—even if we don't think we are at fault. Jesus committed no sin, yet He took all the punishment for sin on our behalf. That is a quality of a true peacemaker.
* Second, if we have an enemy, we ought to love him and give him gifts. It's awfully hard to stay angry with someone who is blessing you with something you can see.
* Third, if there is a deceiver in the group, we put up with him the way Jesus put up with Judas. We are never justified in reacting out of pride. We always have to ask God how to handle it. That takes humility.

God is leading us into a dedicated life, and that is a life that includes a commitment to unity in the body of Christ. All of us who have been redeemed and justified by the blood of Christ are being built up into Him who is the head, Jesus Christ Himself (Ephesians 4:11–16).

Once we understand that, we will begin to grow beyond

our petty jealousies and critical comparisons. We will learn to pray for one another with a power that only God can give. We will be able to "rejoice with those who rejoice, and mourn with those who mourn" (Romans 12:15), meeting the challenges and trials before us as one body of Christ, walking in His likeness.

chapter seven

the greatness of joy

"Then the angel said to them, 'Do not be afraid, for behold, I bring you good tidings of great joy which will be to all people.' " —LUKE 2:10

JESUS SPOKE of many paradoxes in order to explain the spiritual life. One of those paradoxes was "He who finds his life will lose it, and he who loses his life for My sake will find it" (Matthew 10:39). He was telling us that a life of humility is one of great spiritual power. It is also a life of great joy.

A young black woman I know had an experience with losing her life for Jesus' sake and finding a life with the spiritual power of humility when a white shoe store manager in authority over her "seemed to want to see me fail."

"He gave me the worst jobs and expected me to do

everything, while he sat in the office taking the credit," she said.

As much as she didn't want to let him get away with putting her down, she had recently recommitted her life to Christ. So she decided to die to her pride so that God could give her a new life.

"When I was going through this, I was hearing about being a bridge to let others walk on you. There were many days that I had to go to the bathroom and pray for strength to not just walk off the job instead of dealing with this man's stuff," she said. "God said, *Hold on, don't give up. I will give you strength to make it. You will be an example to those who are watching you to see if you will compromise your faith.*

"The more I submitted, the more it seemed like it got worse. Many of the sales associates would ask me why I put up with the manager's demeaning comments and unfair work. I could only say that it would be all over soon. I knew that God had me there for a reason, and until the assignment was over, I'd be right there doing my job as unto the Lord."

After eighteen months of this treatment, she decided to ask for a transfer to a new store that was opening. Her only problem was getting a reference from the troublesome manager. To her surprise, he recommended her highly, and she got the new job. She decided that in the future she would just say it was a learning experience, and not tear down the manager. In the past, she would have been rejoicing at outsmarting the manager, and finally getting free of him, but when she learned to have the mind of Christ in the matter she was able to see him differently. She saw his needs, and she saw her need to be holy. She says, "I am still learning to be the woman that God has intended me to be, daily."

The apostle Timothy reminded us,

> *[F]or if we died with Him,*
> *We shall also live with Him.*
> *If we endure,*
> *We shall also reign with Him*—2 TIMOTHY 2:11, 12.

Salvation starts with death and ends with life, and so does humility. As you die to yourself, a transfer takes place. You lose your life. He gives you His life. It is no longer you who are doing the work, it is Christ. Where you have failed, He succeeds. Where your old, self-centered nature has died, He lives. Instead of remaining a child with all the resentment and rebellion that rule your relationships, you become a spiritually mature adult who is no longer limited by your pride. You are free to be Christ-like. Paul said it a little differently. "It is no longer I who live, but Christ lives in me" (Galatians 2:20).

It is only natural to expect this type of life—the humble life, which requires faith—to be tested. James says that the testing of our faith produces patience (James 1:3). God gives us patience as a fruit of the spirit, but it ripens and matures through His training program—the daily exercise of faith in the midst of trials.

Our first instinct in a trial is to turn from God and return to dependency upon our own resources. Instead of looking to God, we look for our own way out. Instead of surrendering to His will, we rise up and fight. In the face of trials, our natural instinct is to do everything *except* what God tells us to do, which is to "count it all joy" (James 1:2), knowing He will come through in due time. God has to train us to look at life differently. Count it all joy? Yes. God wants us to take each trial and willingly consider it a door to greater faith, peace, and ultimate happiness. Like a banker reckoning accounts, we are to consider our trials as an asset—a blessing—and put them in the "plus" column of our lives. The trials are there to work patience, and patience—when we let it "have its perfect work"—will make us "perfect and complete, lacking nothing" (James 1:4).

I like what England's Benjamin Disraeli said, "Patience is a necessary ingredient of genius."[12] Patience is a place of strength, and it is worked in us through our trials. Trials teach us things that we could never learn in any other way. They prepare us for greatness.

What is left entirely up to us to do is the reckoning—this is, deciding whether or not we will place each trial in the "plus" column as joy, or count trials as debits against us You can't stay focused on your assets when you're focused on your liabilities. The level of joy in your life is a matter of what you emphasize.

More Joy in the Bank

Joy is the fruit of a consecrated life. How can you receive greater joy in your bank account? Consecrate yourself. Set yourself apart for God's use. Change your lifestyle. Change your thought-life. Ask God to help you to find a place of joy in the midst of every circumstance, like an eye in the midst of the storm. If you change your thought-focus to joy, there will be gold in your bank account that keeps shining through the trials, and somebody else will see it and want what is in your account. If nobody is buying your gospel, you may not be showing off anything that is attractive enough to draw them. There is something irresistible about joy.

Joy is knowing that it's not *what* we're going through

that counts with God—it's *how* we're going through it. How we go through a trial depends on the quality of our thought-life.

A focus on changing the thought-life to joy in the midst of trials will help the Church to change a lot of other things. We need to change our ways and take on the ways of the Lord Jesus who died not only to save us but also to change our ways. He has no problem changing our circumstances. One miracle from God could change them in an instant. He does have a problem changing *us*. The problem with Christians is that they have not spent time learning how to think and act like Jesus. When you are born again, your new life is not just a matter of trying to keep from sinning until you get to heaven but of learning how God thinks and how to walk like God in the midst of troubles. Most of us don't want to go through anything we think will make us unhappy. That seems natural. Who wants stress, difficulty, discomfort? Who wants "challenge"? We like everything "quick and easy." As a consequence of this natural aversion to challenges, we avoid doing the will of God whenever it looks as if it will involve something difficult or unpleasant. That is because we tend to see difficulties without seeing God. The devil capitalizes on that. He wants us to look at life's trials with fear and trembling, not joy.

The joy of the Lord is our strength (Nehemiah 8:10). If

we can take each trial and, by the grace of God, place it in the plus column of our lives, we will be able to approach trials in the right spirit. Our strength will grow as our patience is perfected. We will experience peace and joy in the midst of testing.

It is a scientific fact that the exercise of running produces a chemical in a person's system that creates a sense of euphoria. When you start out for a jog, you may not want to do it. Everything inside of you may be saying, "Let's forget this. Let's just go back to bed." However, a few minutes after you start to run, it becomes a joy. You are soaring. Something has been released into your system because you pressed through.

Learning the right approach to trials is not easy. It is like running alone on a cold, dark road while everyone else is asleep. It takes practice to press through to joy. One way we can keep our focus on God's view of our trials and keep our lives overflowing with joy is by spending time with God and His Word. When we fill ourselves with His wisdom and learn His view of things, our faith is fed and our vision grows to become His vision.

Learning how to trust God and His Word is a discipline we choose. It is like choosing to exercise—perhaps difficult and even "unnatural" feeling at first, but in time it yields good results. Paul reminded the church at Philippi to focus on what is true, noble, just, pure, lovely, and of good report, wherever there was any virtue or anything praiseworthy (Philippians 4:8). We need to choose positive thoughts to dominate our thinking, and focus our minds on positive outcomes, knowing that the Lord will work things out. Someone who runs a marathon, for instance, can't focus on how hot he is, or how tired, or how much he wants a drink of water. He has to focus on winning. He has to press when he hits the wall and everything inside of him says, "Stop running!"

We will run well when we can see trials as something that will work out to the glory of God, something that will make us a stronger person who is changed and strengthened by having gone through it. For example, I have always liked sports, so I learned at a young age that if you didn't keep pressing through you could not keep winning. The best athletes are the ones who overcome all of their body's objections and keep on running the race to win.

The benefits of pressing through to joy are guaranteed by the Word of God. Jesus said, "Heaven and earth shall pass away: but my words shall not pass away" (Luke 21:33, KJV). And Peter reminds us of God's words through Isaiah:

" 'All flesh is as grass, and all the glory of man as the
flower of the grass. The grass withers, and its flower

falls away, But the word of the Lord endures forever.' Now this is the word which by the gospel was preached to you"—1 PETER 1:24–25, QUOTING ISAIAH 40:8.

God assures us, "I am watching over My word to perform it" (Jeremiah 1:12, NASB). Where is He performing His Word? In those who establish in their hearts, without changing their minds, that God is real, that He wants the best for you, and that He will be good to keep all of His promises.

Perseverance

Sometimes the only difference between success and failure is the ability to trust God and His promises and persevere in the midst of trials. Usually the strongest people are the ones who have been through all kinds of trials and have still accomplished the purposes they had in mind. Their experience with trials tells them trials don't last forever. The next time they are willing to risk even more, because they have seen that they could endure struggle and hardship—and that this is the way to accomplish great things.

Perseverance comes from a determination we make that we *will* press through, regardless of whatever obstacles we encounter. No matter how many forces come against us, we will take God's view that they are working strength of spirit in us. And make no mistake about it. Perseverance produces results.

In today's Church we are big on results. We like numbers. We measure salvation results in numbers. We measure fund drives in numbers. Although we like to see lives changed in quality, too, we get impatient. We want change to happen quickly. If people struggle or fail, we don't stick around them very long. Maybe our problem is that we don't wait to look at the reasons why our efforts to help them so often fail.

We cannot get the fruits of God until we act in the will of God. The will of God is simply this: obedience. Will we give up when we don't see fruit fast enough in our families, churches, and cities? Or will we press through with people the way God presses through with us?

Peter had a real problem with perserving with people. The Bible says, "Then Peter came to Him and said, 'Lord, how often shall my brother sin against me, and I forgive him? Up to seven times?' Jesus said to him, 'I do not say to you, up to seven times, but up to seventy times seven' " (Matthew 18:21–22).

When you are in school, you have to take tests. If you have the right attitude toward tests in school, you will realize that the test is not to show the teacher how much you know. It is to show *you*. The goal of education is not getting good grades. It is developing mastery of a subject. It is providing you with the tools you need so that you can succeed and you can make a positive contribution to society and the kingdom of God.

God doesn't need to give us a test to show Him how we will respond to a situation. He already knows. He knows all things. God wants *us* to see how we will respond. If we fail the test, He wants us to see that we still have a long way to go in trusting Him, or if we pass, He wants us to see that we have made considerable progress. As we grow, He teaches us more about how to grow deeper and stronger in faith. He teaches us what we need to know to do His work His way.

God is bringing us to the place now where we're not only growing older in years but also older in maturity. Older in wisdom. Older in godliness. He wants us to become spiritual adults. As we grow in spirit, we learn to put all things into perspective. The only ones who never allow God to shape them through trials are those who have not grown up. They are like rebellious toddlers, continually refusing to submit to the will of God. Instead of enduring trials like godly men or women, they fight Him all the way.

Scripture tells us that God has given us everything we

need for life and godliness (2 Peter 1:4). However, we cannot receive this life of power when we are still children. In His awesome grace and mercy, God devises tests that cause us to grow up more quickly so that He can release to us more spiritual authority and power.

Our growth in trials comes as we take our eyes off the natural circumstance; off the trial itself. It also comes as we take our eyes off our own ability—or *lack* of ability—to handle the trial, and fix our eyes on God and His ability. "Set your affection on things above, not on things on the earth. For ye are dead, and your life is hid with Christ in God" (Colossians 3:2–3, KJV).

Catherine Marshall, who was an author, the widow of Peter Marshall (former chaplain of the U.S. Senate), and later the wife of publisher Leonard LeSourd, had to learn as a young mother to focus on things above. When her son was three years old, she was stricken with tuberculosis, and for the next two years was mostly confined to bed. She believed in physical healing, but despite all of her tears she remained an invalid. Finally, she said, she prayed a prayer of surrender. "Lord, I understand no part of this, but if you want me to be an invalid for the rest of my life, well, it's up to You. I place myself in Your hands, for better or for worse. I ask only to serve You."[13]

That was her breakthrough. In the middle of the night,

she said she awakened to find Jesus in the room with her. She wrote, "I knew that Jesus was smiling at me tenderly, lovingly, whimsically—as though a trifle amused at my too-intense seriousness about myself. His attitude seemed to say, 'Relax! There's not a thing wrong here that I can't take care of.'"[14] Then He gave her a simple command, "Go and tell your mother."[15] She knew that she should obey immediately. Even though she didn't want to awaken her, she went to her bedroom and told her, "It's all right. I just want to tell you that I'll be all right now. It seemed important to tell you tonight."[16] And from then on she began to get well. Over her lifetime, the books that she wrote influenced untold multitudes to change their lives and to come to know Jesus in a more personal way. One book, *A Man Called Peter*, was made into a major motion picture after her husband's death, and her novel, *Christy*, became a popular television series. Those are just a few examples of the fruit of a yielded life.

The Bible says that "greater is He that is in us than he that is in the world" (1 John 4:4). As we set our eyes on God, our consciousness becomes greater toward the realities of God, and our fruit proves out our faith in the marketplace.

To grow in spirit and become a mature Christian, subject your senses to God's reality, which is greater than your understanding. "Trust in the LORD with all thine heart; and lean not unto thine own understanding. In all thy ways acknowledge him, and he shall direct thy paths" (Proverbs 3:5–6, KJV). Instead of focusing on your circumstances or the limits of your human ability, or allowing yourself to get frustrated with other people's failures, keep your thoughts on God. He can do the impossible. He can change you, your circumstances, and other people, and He lives inside of you.

Everything God Does Is Eternal

God wants us to focus on the future with eyes of faith because we are being prepared to live with God for time and eternity. The realm of eternity is a whole realm unique to our thinking. Generally we think in the time and space dimension.

One of the keys to emotional stability is learning to live in the realm of eternity. When you have an eternal perspective, problems seem small. You gain control of your attitudes. You develop in character. God approves of your life; not only in time, but also in eternity. You are willing to work for the purposes of God and give your life for what is eternal, instead of surrendering to the tyranny of temporal realities that soon fade away. God wants you to come to the place where you will undertake anything, regardless of the risk, if you believe that God is in it. God wants you to change your tendency to follow your emotions and human senses, and instead follow His will.

Most of us are weak in our faith-vision. We do not know how to keep our eyes fixed on God or the eternal. Because of this, the devil uses our emotional reactions to trials to discourage us from following God. He urges us to give in to fear, which pulls our attention away from our God-given assets. We focus on our lack. To do this is to deny the life of Christ in us. For when we say the trial is too much, we are essentially saying that the eternal life and power of Christ in us is not able to meet the challenge. That is unbelief. That is an insult to God. It is the type of thinking that we used to do before we found Christ. No, giving in to our immediate emotions is not the way to handle a trial. It clouds our vision and blurs our judgment.

Aleksandr Solzhenitsyn, whose life as an underground writer in the Soviet Union was sorely tested by the Communist authorities, understood this principle well. Solzhenitsyn was arrested and spent many years in a Soviet prison camp. Because he had faith in Christ, that faith carried him through those dark days.

For a time, when the political situation eased a bit, he was released and returned home to teach. Still, he remained under the constant scrutiny of a regime that seemed to watch his every move. Faced with the necessity of having to "submit to every bully and acquiesce in every stupidity" of those in authority, he became quite naturally frustrated. The conditions in many ways were no better than the prison camp he had recently left. However, outwardly he remained a model citizen. Meanwhile, his writing, done in secret and carefully hidden, reflected the truth about his situation.

> My indignation could safely boil over in the book I was writing at the time—but I would not allow that either, because the laws of poetry command us to rise above our anger and try to see the present in the light of eternity.[17]

If "the laws of poetry" command such a focus—how much more does "the law of the Spirit of life" ask us to do this? (See Romans 8:1–6.) Solzhenitsyn almost echoes what James has reminded us: Realize that the trials we face have an eternal purpose—a blessing—and will make us complete in every way.

Eternal Life

We are being prepared now to live with God, and the life we are offered is eternal life. If the eternal is not familiar to us, it is because we have grown accustomed to viewing life in terms of the limits of time and space. For example, we manage our daily time in order to take care of priorities at home or on the job. That is in the time and space realm. That is the realm of the Franklin Planner™. We understand that what we are doing today on our job will provide for our tomorrow. If we fulfill the requirements of our employer, we will receive a reward in the form of a paycheck.

It is that way in the earth, but it is also that way in eternity—minus the uncertainty that goes along with depending on people to pay us. With God, there are no uncertainties. The reward is sure. He has already prepared the end for us—life with Him in eternity. We are being prepared now in the time and space realm for life in the realm where God lives and where time is no more.

One of the greatest rewards that God gives us is joy. God has made a way for us to begin living with all the hope and possibility of eternity now. He has given us the ability to refocus our thinking beyond the time and space realm into the realm of the eternal. In this way, we make room for the eternal in us right now. Today.

When we set our minds on the eternal we focus on what is lasting. Everything that God does is lasting. Permanent. He says, "I am the Lord your God. I change not. I am the same yesterday, today, forever" (Malachi 3:6; Hebrews 13:8). Everything God is, and does, and is about is eternal. That is why He wants us to develop a mindset where we think in the eternal realm.

Our training in humility makes us ready for something more than being coworkers with God on earth. It makes us ready to reign with Him in eternity.

Leadership in Eternity

Trials are like a refiner's fire, working out our imperfections. They make us more pure, like God, with whom we are going to reign in heaven. Every one of us needs trials and testing, because we don't know how much of the old snake nature is still in us until somebody steps on us and we strike back. For example, Jesus knew that Peter would betray Him, but Peter didn't. Peter thought he could do anything he set his mind to, but he was wrong. When it came right down to the real trial, Peter gave in to fear. He let go of his reliance on God. He forgot everything that Jesus had taught him.

What we see in Jesus' response is a beautiful picture of

God's refining process. Jesus did not reject Peter. He rebuked him with a look. That was all. And Peter fell apart. He saw himself for what he really was. A betrayer. It was a turning point in Peter's life. He saw himself in a way that he didn't ever want to see himself again, and he changed. The next time he was challenged to deny Jesus, he could not do it. The snake in him was dead. Humility had come alive.

Peter wrote later to others about the joy he was now able to find in his trials. "Beloved, think it not strange concerning the fiery trial which is to try you, as though some strange thing happened unto you: But rejoice, inasmuch as ye are partakers of Christ's sufferings; that, when his glory shall be revealed, ye may be glad also with exceeding joy" (1 Peter 4:12–13, KJV).

Willingness to endure trials with humility is a character quality that God recognizes when He searches the hearts of men and women, looking for someone to lead in His name. Political power and position on earth won't mean a thing in the face of the living God. You may have been a U.S. senator, but unless you sought to be like God, your credentials will not carry over into the realm of heaven. On the other hand you may have held a lowly position that others disdained or overlooked—a janitor or someone who works in the park, or you may have been a prisoner picking up trash on the highway. But if you are surrendered to God you will rule with Him in heaven.

When your heart is humble, it demonstrates that you love God. If you love Him, you value Him and His Word. You are so grateful for what He's done for you that you are willing to do whatever He asks you to do. Your love is demonstrated by your obedience—and He loves and honors you for it. He values you and lifts you up.

The Bible speaks of "the New Jerusalem" that will come down out of heaven. It will be the place from which God rules the re-created heaven and earth. Those in whose hearts God rules and reigns *now*—we *are* the New Jerusalem. We are the bride He is preparing. By training yourself to suffer trials with patience, to learn the humility of Christ, you are making yourself ready now. You are giving up everything for your Divine Husband. Because of all that God has ordained for us in the future, we want to live now at the level of intimacy with God that we will have in heaven. Heaven is the place where we have been ordained to live, both now and in the time to come.

The environment of heaven is characterized by trust and intimacy. As we allow God to create the environment of heaven within us, we prepare ourselves to do His will and rule with His authority. How are we going to reign as God's representatives if we are so weak that we're still controlled by our own will and emotions? This is why God lays His hand on that which we value to test whether or not we value Him more. When a person with wealth really gives himself to the Lord, he gives God control of all of his earthly substance. He transfers over to God everything that brought him honor in the world in order to receive a higher honor in heaven. He wants to be accepted by God more than he wants to be accepted by men. God will test you when it comes to wealth—not just money—but intelligence, talent, a position of respect or power, or your family.

How do we give of our "wealth"? We give to His work—whatever will accomplish God's purposes. We give all we have so that the knowledge of God spreads throughout the earth. When we give we are saying to God, "I am demonstrating my willingness to submit to you for all eternity by being in subjection to you now." If we hold back from giving everything to the Lord now, we should not deceive ourselves into thinking we will be able to give everything to God in eternity. God says His will shall be done on earth as it is in heaven. We can't fool God. The truth is, if we hold back and postpone our submission to God, we will not be ready to do His will and His work in heaven. Our hearts will be unprepared for that kind of intimacy. When God plays back the recording of our lives to us, we will hear again every word we said, every thought, and every deed, and we will be so sorry that we did not submit everything to Him. We will know that we could have had even greater rewards in heaven, but we failed the test that God gave us on earth.

I want to be among the ones to whom the Lord says, "Well done, thy good and faithful servant." Don't you? Now is the hour for the true Church—the body of Christ on earth—to come forth. We need to ask God to change us so that we will become like Christ in our surrender and faithfulness to God. We will become like Him in our giving. We will become like Him in our mercy and love. Before the foundation of the world, God saw our heart as good ground, and so He sent Christ to be our example so that we could become like Him.

All of us are on a pilgrimage to the eternal city of God. We are preparing ourselves now to enter that place where God alone will rule all things again. God doesn't value gold and silver. He has all of the gold at His disposal. He values people. He has created us for Himself. He longs for those who have not yet made room for Him in their hearts. He values those who are willing to be transformed into the image of His humble Son, so that He may share all of eternity with us.

We have a vacuum in leadership in this generation.

People are looking for leaders who have the power to make things happen yet still possess the character to keep themselves from falling into sin. That is the kind of power that God demonstrates through His yielded people in the earth.

Jesus is praying for our success. In Ephesians 3:20 the Bible says, "Now unto him that is able to do exceeding abundantly above all that we ask or think, according to the power that worketh in us, Unto him be glory in the church by Christ Jesus throughout all ages, world without end. Amen" (Ephesians 3:20–21, KJV).

Is God's power going to work? Yes it is going to work, but where will it work? It is working now in us. God's power at work in us is not measurable. He blesses us beyond measure. He is able to do exceedingly abundantly above all that you can ask or think. He can make you into any kind of leader He wants. If you will yield to Him as the great Master Craftsman, He will take you beyond every limitation and every failure of the past, because He is God. He is giving us strength to carry the cross, so we will have the authority that comes from humility to wear the crown.

chapter eight

the low road to leadership

D O YOU CONSIDER yourself a leader or a future leader? Do you know how to become a leader after God's own heart? The man whom the Bible described as a leader after God's own heart was David, the king of Israel: "I have found David the son of Jesse, a man after My own heart, who will do all My will" (Acts 13:22).

David took the low road to leadership. The youngest of the sons of Jesse, he tended sheep alone in the fields. He was not even invited when the prophet Samuel came to visit the home. When he went to take provisions to his brothers who were fighting the Philistines, they mocked him when he asked questions about the giant Goliath—until he killed him.

When David was called upon to serve King Saul, through no fault of his own the king turned against him and flew into rages, eventually trying to kill David, who ran for his life and lived in caves with a ragtag band of men who followed him. While he was in the wilderness, he and his men helped protect the property of a man named Nabal, but all he received in return was ridicule and rejection.

Eventually Saul died and David became king, but because he had taken the low road to leadership he was a different kind of king from Saul. He had such a humble heart toward God that even when he turned away from God's ways and sinned with Bathsheba, when the prophet Nathan confronted him he broke down and repented. He was not a rebel like Saul, who sinned and made excuses. He was a child who knew that His Father's way was the right way. Are you?

David's kingdom lasted and flourished. He presided over a golden age for Israel full of wealth and peace with other nations. God is looking for people like David who have humble hearts so that He can make them into leaders who last. He is getting ready to transfer leadership from the Sauls, those men who stand head and shoulders above the people of our day (1 Samuel 9:2), to the Davids—those who would ordinarily be ignored by people who look only at outward signs of greatness (1 Samuel 16:7).

If we go after God's own heart, as David did, God will give us oversight over people, regardless of how humble our circumstances are now. The only people God can trust to be leaders are those who want to please Him. David pleased Him some of the time, and disappointed Him at other times, but we have someone to follow who always pleased the Father—Jesus. Ultimately we will rule with Jesus over kingdoms and nations in eternity, but right now we are learning to be like Him by learning how to rule our own spirits in our homes and churches and in the marketplace. We are preparing to take our places of authority on the earth in this present world, and our places of authority in the world to come.

Christians have a leadership role to play on the earth, and creation itself is waiting for us to come into our rightful place. Ever since the Fall, all the earth has suffered because of Adam's sin. The second Adam came to redeem us and change us so that we could reclaim the earth and restore it to its state before the Fall.

For I consider that the sufferings of this present time are not worthy to be compared with the glory that is to be revealed to us. For the anxious longing of the creation waits eagerly for the revealing of the sons of God. For the creation was subjected to futility, not of its own will, but because of Him who subjected it, in hope that the creation itself also will be set free from its slavery to corruption into the freedom of the glory of the children of God. For we know that the whole creation groans and suffers the pains of childbirth together until now —ROMANS 8:18–22, NASB.

God wants us to be leaders, and we train for leadership God's way by learning how to be humble. When Christians attain positions by earthly methods and demand that people respect them and call them by the right title, they are out of divine order. They have the "pride of grace"—they are proud of something that they did nothing to deserve. They are not responsible for their salvation, because grace is unmerited favor, and they are not responsible for the position, because God sets one up and puts another down.

Pride in any form is not a character quality of Christ, yet you know that some pastors speaking to tens of thousands of people let that pride slip in there. You don't need thousands of members in your church to qualify as a leader after God's own heart. You just need to know how great He is and how little you can accomplish without Him.

True leaders are people who keep trying to please God.

When they fail to please Him, they don't give up. They see failure not as a stumbling block but as a stepping stone. That takes a type of death to self. When you make a big mistake, or if you really blow it and sin and have to repent, as David did, you have to die to what others think about you and live only for the approval of God.

Jesus said, "Most assuredly, I say to you, unless a grain of wheat falls into the ground and dies, it remains alone; but if it dies, it produces much grain. He who loves his life will lose it, and he who hates his life in this world will keep it for eternal life" (John 12:24–25). Every Christian has to die to himself before he can live in newness of life, because the Holy Spirit doesn't raise anything that is not dead. That is the death/life principle—the way to new life is death to the old life. "Now if we died with Christ, we believe that we shall also live with Him, knowing that Christ, having been raised from the dead, dies no more" (Romans 6:8–9).

A soldier with no fear of death has a great advantage in a war. An athlete with no fear of death to self has a great advantage in a race. If you are an Olympic runner, you might fear making a public spectacle of yourself by falling on the track. You might be afraid that you would make it all the way to the Olympics, then as you are racing down the track and the crowd is cheering all of a sudden you trip on your own feet and fall flat on your face halfway through the race. That is a pride-killer. But what kind of runner do we admire most? The one who is not afraid to run, and then if he falls he gets back on his feet and finishes, even if he finishes dead last and the rest of the competition has already gone to the showers.

The True Leader's Training

God is looking for men and women who will run the race for souls—the great spiritual leaders this generation needs. How does one identify true spiritual leaders? You can see the hand of God on their lives in their humility, sacrifice, and commitment to serve those under them as well as those above them. When you are with them, you sense something genuine. You don't have the feeling that they are smiling to your face and putting you down behind your back. When you're in trouble, they are there for you. If you backslide, they forgive you—maybe with some strong fatherly advice on what you did wrong and how to change and do better the next time, but always with a grace and humility that doesn't put you down permanently.

The Bible is full of examples of people like David, who took the low road to leadership. Their preparation for leadership was not domination but humiliation. Before they came to power, they had trials that taught them perseverance. Here are a few other biblical examples:

Moses, the adopted son of Pharaoh's daughter, killed an Egyptian soldier to protect one of his Israelite people, but had to run for his life and live in the wilderness because his pride and impulsive sin had thrown him out of God's will. God had to break him before He could use him. Moses remained for the next forty years as a shepherd in submission to his father-in-law, Jethro, before God could trust him with true authority over Israel.

Nehemiah was a slave of the king of Persia, and served as his cup bearer—the man who tested the king's food and drink before the king did in case it contained poison. God used Nehemiah's humble position to get him close enough to the king to speak on behalf of his people, the Jews. Eventually he became their governor and rebuilt Jerusalem. After rising to power God's way, the way of humility, no ridicule or threats from his enemies could deter him from his God-appointed task.

Nebuchadnezzar was already a powerful ruler before God humbled him, but he still had to come up another level. Nebuchadnezzar had a serious problem. He refused to acknowledge God as the supreme authority of everything in heaven and on earth. He refused to give honor to the one true God for raising him up as a king. He took all the credit to himself, saying, "Is not this great Babylon, that I have built for a royal dwelling by my mighty power and for the honor of my majesty?" (Daniel 4:30).

With that attitude, Nebuchadnezzar met the opposition of God. Even as he was speaking, his judgment was pronounced by a voice from heaven. "[T]he kingdom has departed from you!" (Daniel 4:31). Nebuchadnezzar's downfall was startling. From his symptoms, we'd say he went mad. For the next seven years he "ate grass like oxen; his body was wet with the dew of heaven till his hair had grown like eagles' feathers and his nails like birds' claws" (Daniel 4:33).

After years of such humiliation, revelation finally came to him. In Nebuchadnezzar's words:

> And at the end of the time I, Nebuchadnezzar, lifted my eyes to heaven, and my understanding returned to me; and I blessed the Most High and praised and honored Him who lives forever: for His dominion is an everlasting dominion, and His kingdom is from generation to generation. All the inhabitants of the earth are reputed as nothing; he does according to His will in the army of heaven and among the inhabitants of the earth. No one can restrain His hand or say to Him, "What have You done?"

At the same time my reason returned to me, and for the glory of my kingdom, my honor and splendor returned to me. My counselors and nobles resorted to me, I was restored to my kingdom, and excellent majesty was added to me. Now I, Nebuchadnezzar, praise and extol and honor the King of heaven, all of whose works are truth, and His ways justice. And those who walk in pride He is able to put down—DANIEL 4:34–37.

Godly and Ungodly Leadership

Do you know how to recognize when your thinking is going the way of Nebuchadnezzar and leading you into pride and improper attitudes on the road to leadership? When you are striving unsuccessfully for leadership and continually frustrated in your ambition to obtain power, do you know where to look for the real obstacles? Do you remain steady in prayer and worship, confident of victory even when you feel weak and intimidated? Do you have the godly confidence of a David or a Moses, or do you feel inside the agitation of frustration, fear, and defeat of a prideful Nebuchadnezzar?

Some of the greatest threats we face come from within. Many Christians defeat themselves with self-condemnation or self-exaltation. They give in to anger, doubt, criticism, and fear. Leaders have to be so surrendered to God that His strength sustains them and gives them confidence in the face of all obstacles. When God is leading them, then they can lead others.

People seeking power the ungodly way take opportunities to get even with their enemies. They harbor grudges in their hearts and wait for the moment of revenge when they can strike back. Jesus was not like that. With Judas in the midst of the disciples, He maintained the character of a godly leader. He never lost His sense of regality. People who seek revenge are children, not leaders. They lack reverence for God, who says that He will avenge all offenses, the Lord who deals personally with all who need correction, and ultimately deals also with those who take their own revenge.

> Beloved, do not avenge yourselves, but rather give place to wrath; for it is written, "Vengeance is Mine, I will repay," says the Lord. Therefore "If your enemy is hungry, feed him; if he is thirsty, give him a drink; for in so doing you will heap coals of fire on his head. Do not be overcome by evil, but overcome evil with good"
> —ROMANS 12:19.

Godly people do not start smear campaigns. David didn't do it. Even though Saul was his enemy, David respected his authority. David did not condone Saul's behavior, but he did respect the man whom God had put in place as king.

David knew what many spiritual leaders do not know, or else they forget. Authority comes from God. That is why the Bible exhorts us to pray for those in authority. "I exhort therefore, that, first of all, supplications, prayers, intercessions, and giving of thanks, be made for all men; For kings, and for all that are in authority; that we may lead a quiet and peaceable life in all godliness and honesty" (1 Timothy 2:1–2, KJV).

Naturally, we resist the idea of having someone "over" us—someone having the authority to approve or veto what we want. Most of us, though we won't admit it, would prefer to lord it over others. However, by honoring authority we honor God and contribute to our own peaceful living. God has set *authority* itself in place for His divine purpose. He uses authority figures—good or bad, saint or sinner—to work many things into our character. What he was working in David was *brokenness* and *restraint*, training him in the very traits needed for spiritual leadership.

Before David could reign as a king, he had to be broken of any desire for his promised kingship. He had to learn the mature restraint that is necessary to wait upon God, so that God can unfold His plan in His way and in His time. Once again, the way to life is death—death to our own way, but alive and obedient to the way of God. That is what

Abraham Lincoln had to experience, and so have many others who have made it to the top.

An Obedient Heart

Eventually, Scripture tells us, God rejected Saul as king. Saul did not have a heart for God. He had a heart for Saul. He compromised and disobeyed God. Even after the prophet Samuel told Saul that God had rejected him as king, Saul still wanted to be honored by men. This shows he had no idea of the enormity of what he had done. He never took sin seriously. Saul said to Samuel, "I have sinned: yet *honour me now*, I pray thee, before the elders of my people, and before Israel, and turn again with me, that I may worship the LORD thy God" (1 Samuel 15:30, KJV, italics added by author).

The honor of men means nothing when we do not have the honor that comes from God alone. God honors us when we obey. He does not force us to obey Him, but He fully expects us to obey. We often think of disobedience in the terms of committing overt sin. Actually, God's requirement goes to a much deeper level than that. When God tells us to do something, we who consider ourselves leaders must be ready to act on His words, immediately, if necessary. If He speaks and we delay because we are calculating whether or not our actions will be approved or disapproved by others, we prove we are worshipping the honor of men and not the true God. Pride is ruling us. We have moved onto the ground of disobedience. Our only hope is that the fear of God will come on us, and we will obey regardless of the cost to our approval rating with people!

Obedience requires us to listen attentively to God. Saul's place of authority was taken from him when he did not comply with God's requirements, refusing to do God's will in destroying the Amalekites. God's will was to bring retribution upon the Amalekites for what they had done to Israel during their passage out of Egypt. God had commanded Saul to destroy everything that the Amalekites had, which included men, women, children, ox and cattle. Saul, however, got into a state many leaders recognize—analysis paralysis. As he thought about the situation, he decided he knew more than God. And so he spared some of the Amalekites and kept some of the booty God wanted destroyed. He let God's people become common things, focusing on their gain, rather than keeping them focused on their holy purpose.

To act in the name of God and then do our own will is a terrible thing. Christian leaders do it. Some of the most rebellious and stubborn people I know are in the pulpit. If we are not careful to live in the lowly spirit of Christ, we rise up and try to have our own way. Focusing on our purposes, we become disobedient to the purposes of God. However, once we come to Jesus in a real way, all of that foolishness has to stop, because the Church must get on with the work of the kingdom in this generation. And so, we who would prepare ourselves for leadership must learn to restrict ourselves, as David did. We must not give in to our personal kingdom-building impulses. We must restrain ourselves from using our natural abilities for self-promotion. There is only one way to overcome disobedience. That is by being obedient. We have to do whatever it takes to obey God.

Somewhere inside each of us is the impulse to build a lasting memorial. Too often, our efforts are bent toward building a memorial to our own greatness, rather than to the glory of God. It's interesting that God never allowed David to build a magnificent temple for the ark. He was prohibited because of the sins he had committed. But God did use him to prepare the finances for the temple He would ask Solomon to build. And yet, because David was a man after God's own heart, God used him and released through him many spiritual blessings.

Saul was a king after the flesh. David was a king after the spirit. He had learned in the caves to restrict his flesh; that is, to restrict his motivations that were fleshly, while releasing his motivations that were spiritual. He saw that the initiative for each breakthrough would have to come by the spirit of God. He learned what Saul never learned—to consult God, and let God set the conditions and terms. It is then that the release of power, the breakthrough, comes.

> So David went to Baal Perazim, and David defeated them there; and he said, "The LORD has broken through my enemies before me, like a breakthrough of water." Therefore he called the name of that place Baal Perazim
> —2 SAMUEL 5:20.

Restoring the People to God

What is the breakthrough you are looking for in this generation? The breakthrough of revival affects leaders. It is the release of God's Spirit into the world, to the people of the world, those who are still living and dying trapped in the old nature of the snake. It is more than an experience. Any one of us can say, "I know Christ. He's in me." We need a spiritual transformation so deep that we lay down our lives for all the people of this generation.

If you are seeking change or spiritual growth just so that you feel good about yourself, you are on the wrong track.

You are headed for self-righteousness. God transforms us into the lowly image of Christ for a reason that is beyond our individuality. First He changes us, then, as instruments of His gentleness, meekness, patience, love, and kindness, His Spirit in us changes others.

Because God knew David would give his life for the sake of all the people, God raised him to leadership. God said, "I have found David the son of Jesse, a man after My own heart, who will do *all* My will" (Acts 13:22, italics added by author). Under Saul, the Ark of the Covenant, which represented the presence of God, was lost. Saul himself had lost God's presence. The first thing David did after becoming king was to bring back the Ark of the Covenant, restoring the people to the leadership of the Holy Spirit. David recognized worship as essential because it would focus Israel back on God, not on a political leader. He knew the people needed healing in spirit and restoration to God. This is a lesson for all us would-be spiritual leaders. True purpose and vision must be restored first—to us and to the people under us. When we can get *God's* direction, then we can properly tend His sheep.

When our old nature, that which rises up to seek our own benefit, is dealt with, we take on the lowly quality of a leader who has been qualified by God. What is that quality? Mercy. In the words of the prophet Isaiah, "For *in mercy* shall the throne be established: and he shall sit upon it in truth in the tabernacle of David, judging, and seeking judgment, and hasting righteousness" (Isaiah 16:5, KJV, italics added by author).

It is significant that Isaiah places the throne within the tabernacle—the tent of meeting where the Ark of the Covenant rested, where the people of Israel came before the presence of the living God. David knew this was where he wanted to be, and needed to be. It was a place of humility—where sin was forgiven, and mercy received. And it was there David learned the quality of mercy so necessary to become a leader after God's own heart.

Mercy is a natural result of being in God's presence, just like joy. Godly leaders are merciful, because in the presence of God they stand broken, knowing they themselves are received in mercy. Mercy draws us to the throne of grace and keeps us coming back. We become sensitive to sin in our own lives, but when we address it in the lives of others, there will be compassion in our voice and mercy in our hearts.

It is easy to think that righteousness will be more efficiently accomplished through judgment, but often this amounts to little more than our harsh and insensitive condemnation of others. When we stop judging the people in our care, we become vessels of mercy, and we hasten righteousness.

Mercy is not weakness. It is strength and wisdom, the hallmark of a leader trained in humility. One of the fruits of mercy is joy. Have you ever seen a really serious sinner get saved? How did you feel? Did you rejoice as Jesus said heaven rejoices (Luke 15:7)? Mercy is a lot more fun than judgment. It's a great joy.

chapter nine

preparing to move forward

I WANT TO CLOSE this book by challenging you to take what you have learned about pleasing God with a lifestyle of humility and move forward into all that God has prepared for you as His child. The possibilities are awesome. "Eye hath not seen, nor ear heard, neither have entered into the heart of man, the things which God hath prepared for them that love him. But God hath revealed them unto us by his Spirit" (1 Corinthians 2:9–10, KJV).

The secret to knowing where and when to move forward in God's will is becoming the kind of person whom God can direct by His Holy Spirit. That's what this book has been about. In the Old Testament, people moved forward when they saw outward manifestations of the Holy Spirit. The presence of God was visible. The Israelites moved forward because they saw the cloud move.

> And the Lord went before them by day in a pillar of a cloud, to lead them the way; and by night in a pillar of fire, to give them light; to go by day and night: He took not away the pillar of the cloud by day, nor the pillar of fire by night, from before the people—Exodus 13:21–22, KJV.

At the outpouring of the Holy Spirit at Pentecost, God began to move people in a new way, by the inward sense of His presence. No matter where we are or what we are doing, if we want to know where God wants us to move next, we should have one main thought: "Is God with me?"

If you don't have a sense of His presence and you can't comprehend His will, your next question should be this: "Is there anything about my life that is displeasing to God?" Pleasing God is the key to hearing from God, because God is only going to be where it pleases Him to be. God isn't led by us; we are led by God.

If you want to maintain a sense that God is with you, live

in such a way that you are willing to do whatever it takes to please Him. One of the most important ways that you can please God is by living a lifestyle of humility. God loves humility. He hates the proud look (see Proverbs 6:16–17). A high look is sin (see Proverbs 21:4). "God resists the proud, but gives grace to the humble" (James 4:6).

You are alive today because God needs you to reach this generation for Him. This is a proud and prosperous generation, a self-sufficient generation of people who are not interested in the true and living God. They think they don't need Him to save them. They think they can save themselves. These are the people God is calling us to reach with our humility.

> There is a generation that curses its father, and does not bless its mother. There is a generation that is pure in its own eyes, yet is not washed from its filthiness. There is a generation—oh, how lofty are their eyes! And their eyelids are lifted up. There is a generation whose teeth are like swords, and whose fangs are like knives, to devour the poor from off the earth, and the needy from among men—PROVERBS 30:11–14.

Do you want to identify with this generation and follow their ungodly lifestyles, or are you willing to identify with Jesus and die to everything else so that you can truly live?

Israel's pillar of fire was a point of demarcation between Egypt, which was behind them, and Israel, the people led by God. The fire represents God's intensity, and the separation of His people from the world. The fire also represents your intensity for God. You are intense to the level that you experience His reality. The fire represents your consecration, purging out of you all of the pride and other sins that keep you from His presence.

God is looking for a few consecrated people who, like the sons of Issachar with David at Ziklag, understand the times, and know what they ought to do (see 1 Chronicles 12:32). Humble people of God are about to be set into positions of power. They may not know it yet, but God is preparing them for greatness.

How do we prepare for greatness? Jesus told us that greatness comes about through weakness. When Jesus died, the world saw Him as weak. The devil was fooled into thinking that He won. But Jesus Christ died to make us strong. With His death, a way is provided for us to die to ourselves and be resurrected into a new life. "The body is sown in corruption, it is raised in incorruption. It is sown in dishonor, it is raised in glory. It is sown in weakness, it is raised in power. It is sown a natural body, it is raised a spiritual body" (1 Corinthians 15:42–44).

Today, around the world, there is a sense of great excitement among Christian leaders anticipating a new groundswell of the Holy Spirit. What we have witnessed of God's glory, what we have experienced of the Spirit's saving, healing ministry—these things will hardly compare with the outpouring works of God that He wants to visit upon the earth. The time is growing nearer every day.

One of God's greatest mercies is that He shares His glory with us, pouring His very life into human vessels. We were created in His image, but in order to share in the fullness of God's Spirit, as we have seen, we must set aside the old nature that rises up for its own glory and humbly empty ourselves before Him.

Jesus told us to cultivate greatness through weakness. Those who rule in His kingdom are those who practice vulnerability. Do whatever it takes to submit yourself to God, so that His Spirit is in control of your inmost being. Every one of us will need intense concentration in the challenges that are about to come. For just as the Holy Spirit is to be poured out in greater measure, greater forces of evil than you can imagine are about to move against us. Only those who are weak in themselves and strong in the Lord will be strong. As Scripture tells us, "[T]hey who seek the LORD shall not be in want of any good thing" (Psalm 34:10, NASB).

God is looking for people with whom He can share His

power who will use that power *for His purposes, not theirs*. God doesn't give power for the purpose of self-exaltation or for the development of personal agendas.

As we have seen, God does not look for "perfect" people with whom to share His glory and power. David was far from perfect. But he was lowly in heart. Most of the time, he chose not to use his power irresponsibly, or for his own personal exaltation. And even though David went through long years of abasement, and times of humiliation, God had set a timetable for David's promotion—a promotion from God and for God's purposes.

David was in power so that he could fulfill God's purposes. That is the way it must be with us. Not one goal that you and I choose on our own is acceptable before God. As we have seen, our responsibility is to submit to the goals God has chosen for us.

Sons of Issachar

To stay focused on the task at hand—that is, to prepare ourselves to be the vessels of God's outpouring—will require great focus. We are surrounded by prophets with worldly wisdom. The shallowness of worldly wisdom is that it focuses on our selfish ambitions. What we can have. What we can be. How we can exalt ourselves in mind, body, and position. The "human potential" movement is at its peak. Where is the consideration of eternity? Everybody wants a word of advice about the "*now*." Wall Street rises and falls on every little breath of the economic forecast. In our own personal schedules, we think about "getting out the door" and on to "the next thing." In our busyness we leave no time for reflection. Everyone is looking for direction, with little thought that what we truly need is the guidance that comes from outside time—from eternity.

Even in the Church we are looking for someone who "knows what God is up to." And while we need the voice of the prophet, and the pastor, it is time for each of us to ask "What is my responsibility?" "What am I to do?" "Where will God have me to serve as He unfolds His magnificent plan for the ages?" Only those who have surrendered themselves to God will be given wisdom to grasp the answers to these questions. For wisdom is the insight God sets in the hearts of those who are at rest under His authority—those who are awake in the Spirit, alert and listening and watching for the movements of God Himself, so they can follow Him and do what He is doing.

Today, God is preparing a generation of people who are wise in the things of God. Are you one of them? Those whom God is preparing will be like the sons of Issachar, who had an "understanding of the times, to know what

Israel ought to do" (1 Chronicles 12:32). An "understanding of the times" does not just mean possessing a plan of action for the immediate future. It implies an awareness of God's movements, so that we can have a context from which to view current events. To get that perspective we need to spend time with God and His Word. These were leaders who had direction, not just for themselves, but for the nation.

There were four sons of Issachar: Tola, Puah, Jashub, and Shimron (1 Chronicles 7:1). Each of these names has great prophetic significance for our calling to Christlikeness and our preparation to serve the world in His name. They represent the characteristics of those who are spiritually sensitive to what God is about to do. They speak of qualities we must develop in order to serve under God's authority as ambassadors to this world today.

Let us examine these names, and consider the character qualities God wants to create in us.

Tola

The name of the first son of Issachar, Tola, means "worm." Keep in mind the Hebrew tradition was to name children for the traits or character qualities you saw in them or wished for them to emulate. And so we have to ask, why would you give your son a name like that? It doesn't sound like a good choice at first, but *tola* was the word for a certain type of worm that yielded a precious dye. The crimson it produced was used to make the most costly and beautiful garments of the day. Because of their value, these colors were associated with royalty. Only kings and queens wore clothes dyed with the crimson and scarlet of the *tola*.

Ironic, isn't it, that a worm would produce the thing that marked someone with royal honor and position? What is of greater interest to us is that this same word—*tola*—is also used in Psalm 22, the great messianic psalm of David we quoted in the first chapter. David prophesies the words Jesus would utter on the cross and they describe the attitude of spirit that led Him to that sacrificial moment: "But I am a worm, and no man; a reproach of men, and despised of the people" (Psalm 22:6). What is it that marks Jesus' spiritual exaltation: His holy royalty? It is the crimson of His shed blood. For He who humbled Himself like a worm and became obedient to suffer death on a cross, is now highly exalted, "that at the name of Jesus every knee should bow, of those in heaven, and of those on earth, and of those under the earth, and that every tongue should confess that Jesus Christ is Lord, to the glory of God the Father" (Philippians 2:10–11).

"Jesus was obedient even unto death." (Philippians 2:8,

KJV). Do we who call ourselves the children of God, the followers of Jesus, grasp what this means? Do we consider every day what type of spirit must be in us if we are truly to be followers of Jesus Christ and call Him our Lord? Jesus was not on the cross because He was forced to be on it, but because He submitted Himself to it. He became a man for us, but not a self-exalting man. He became a man of the lowest kind—a slave (see Philippians 2:7). Like a slave, He held no rights of His own. He came in the name of His master, to do the will of the One who sent Him. His work was obedience.

As we have seen all along, the nature that was in Christ—lowliness—must be in us. And if we are going to be the wisdom of God to our generation, we must be willing to show them how to find the only life that matters—eternal life. Like Christ we must be willing to become the lowliest so that others might have life. For as Jesus said, "He who finds his life will lose it, and he who loses his life for My sake will find it" (Matthew 10:39). The mark of our royalty in God is that we live under the crimson blood of Jesus. That blood and our testimony make us overcomers—more than conquerors—if we refuse to love our own life more than doing the will of God (see Revelation 12:11).

God is calling us to submit ourselves to be used by Him in whatever place He sends us. So many have emphasized that the Christian needs to find his or her gifts or calling, but that is out of order. Until we submit to His authority and take our place as servants, He cannot reveal the greatest mystery, which is Christ in us, to the world. Neither will God entrust us with gifts, callings, or revelations until we die to our self-centeredness, because with these things comes responsibility. That is the responsibility of lifting up others by the Spirit until they, too, see God and worship Him and follow Him.

There is no greater burden than our self. This is why we must lay our self down, and leave the area of our rights and needs to God. Jesus did not carry a burden for Himself. He lived to fulfill the purposes of God. Most of us want to get rid of the circumstances that we are experiencing, but if we leave our cares to God, we receive grace to lift others' burdens. It is then that we find the joy that Jesus found when God empowered Him with the Spirit to pour out His soul for others.

God's word to us who claim to serve in His name is this: We are to sacrifice our burdensome lives into His care—for He *will* care for us—and to take up His burden for the whole world.

Puah

The next son of Issachar was named Puah. It means *to blow away*, or *to scatter*. This too has prophetic significance for us today.

Just before returning to the heavenly Father, Jesus gave His disciples authority to perform a very great task. We are to go into all the world and preach the Gospel—the good news about what Jesus Christ has done to save the world from sin. If we go out in His Spirit, having lain down our worldly lives, we become living witnesses to the fact that we are redeemed through His blood. The disciples were to become apostles—the "sent out" ones. They did not fully act upon the authority they were given, though, until they were persecuted and scattered.

God's Word to us is that we must be willing to be scattered by God wherever His Spirit will send us. Two millennia ago, Jesus commissioned His disciples to carry the Gospel to every part of the world. Much has been accomplished by those who have gone before us. They have made great sacrifices, but there is still much more to be done. The authority to make disciples of all nations was not given to just a few. It was given to all of us who are followers of Jesus. Just like the first disciples of Christ, we have been given power through the Holy Spirit, whose name also means *wind*. He is the very breath of God—the wind that will lift us out of our comfortable lives and take us as messengers of the good news to the four corners of the earth.

Many have gone out in the name of God, but not in the uplifting power of the Spirit of God. Some have returned discouraged. God's plan was never for us to work on our own. We are to take the Gospel by the impartation of the Holy Spirit. After the Holy Ghost has come upon you, you receive power to be his witnesses "to the uttermost parts of the earth" (Acts 1:8). The word that is translated "power" is *dunamis*, a Greek word whose root is also used in the word dynamite. The word translated "witnesses" is from a Greek word that means martyr. It is only when we die to ourselves that our lives bear witness of Christ in us.

When we receive the dynamite blast of the Holy Spirit on the inside of us, we will be scattered to the four corners of the earth to demonstrate with our lives that Christ lives. That is the will of the Father who loved the whole world enough to send His Son for the sake of the whole world.

Have you ever seen a gathering of dust in a little pile and blown on it with just a little puff of breath? How easily it scatters. That is the way we will be when we become lowly before God. He will blow on us by the Spirit and we will go wherever He blows. For then we will be sensitive enough to the heart of the Father to be easily directed.

Jashub

Jashub, the third prophetic name among the sons of Issachar, means *he that will return*. It means to turn back or withdraw in order to restore, rescue, or retrieve. God says that we are called to restore the desolation that has come to us from former generations (Isaiah 58:12).

In past generations, Christianity became a matter of outward form and ritual. God is restoring to us today the truth that we may experience direct fellowship and communion with Him. As we draw aside to Him in our prayer closets, His Spirit grows strong in us. His visitation will come through people who have received in prayer, by the Spirit, a divine sense of calling to go out, carrying the presence of the Lord with them. What is it that we are restoring? We are rebuilding the old, foundational truths that have lain in ruins, forgotten. The righteous are withdrawing into the closets of prayer so that they can be restored by God. They are retrieving what was lost by the desolation of the palmerworm, cankerworm, caterpillar, and locust (see Joel 1). The ones who will do this are those who have withdrawn from the company of people to be alone with God, to know His heart. They are the ones who go beyond the "form" of Christianity because they are filled with the Holy Spirit and long to do God's will. And so the breath of God will scatter them where they are to go.

Shimron

Shimron, the fourth prophetic name we must consider, means *to guard*. It means to protect or tend, to be circumspect, or mature. And it also implies maturity, like a wine that has aged well. Today, God is calling us to handle great truths. Before He can trust us with great truths, He first has to mature us.

The Bible says, "The glory of young men is their strength" (Proverbs 20:29, KJV). Usually when a new Christian gets some spiritual understanding, the first thing he wants to do is run out and say and do the first thing that comes to mind. But when this impulsiveness passes, nothing of lasting value has been accomplished.

We are to become settled and mature, "men of war, *that could keep rank*" (1 Chronicles 12:38, KJV, italics added by author). We are to let God put us in whatever rank He chooses. God is the Appointer. We are the appointees. "For promotion cometh neither from the east, nor from the west, nor from the south. But God is the judge: he putteth down one, and setteth up another" (Psalm 75:6–7, KJV).

Some leaders in the body of Christ today have not subdued their independent spirit. They want to go their own way and do their own thing. They are not team players. They want to be captain or they won't play. Not everyone is called to be a captain in the ranks of God, even those who are mature in spirit. Some of us are called to be in the squad. The important thing is for us to have a perfect heart wherever we are called to serve. If we can keep rank and have a perfect heart, we will not care about getting promoted to the next position.

What the sons of Issachar and the other men who joined David cared about was helping him to receive the kingdom that had been promised to him by God.

Is Jesus King?

Is it the desire of your heart to see the kingdom of all mankind restored to Christ? Or is it your design to set yourself up with your own rights so you can rule over your own patch of ground? We can tell whether or not we are standing in God's ranks by what is in our hearts. Do we have a desire to uplift Jesus and see others come to worship Him as Lord? Is He at the center of our lives? It's not a matter of uplifting our pastor, our church, our denomination. Certainly not ourselves. It's a matter of whether or not we are lifting up the Lord Jesus Christ.

Jesus came to the earth as Savior and Prophet. He is now ministering before the right hand of God as Intercessor, or Priest. He shall soon return as King. We are gathering around the Lord Jesus as the men gathered around David. They wanted to make David king, and we want to make Jesus King. We do that as we allow Him to be *Adonai*—Lord and Master—over our own hearts and lives. Others will see and want to make Him Lord and king, too, as we exalt Him in our lives. He said, "And I, if I be lifted up from the earth, will draw all men unto me" (John 12:32, KJV).

Who is Jesus going to use in this last day? Those people who are lifting Him up. Right now He is drawing them to Himself. Where is it that He Himself has been raised up? He dwells with God the Father in heavenly places. By lifting up Jesus, we, too, are raised up in spirit. And though life throws every hardship at us, within us it can be heaven.

This Final Hour

Let me tell you what's going to happen to those of us whom God is raising up in this hour. . . .

Peter, after the outpouring of the Holy Spirit, began to preach a great message that is for us today. He said to the crowds, "Repent ye therefore, and be converted, that your sins may be blotted out, when the times of refreshing shall come from the presence of the Lord" (Acts 3:19, KJV). The Holy Spirit had just been poured out, but Peter gave the crowds a prophetic message, telling them to repent and be converted. If they did so, he said they could be a part of the times of refreshing that were going to come. Today is that time. Now is that hour. New times of refreshing are coming from the presence of the Lord. We are to draw closer and closer to Him. First, through repentance, and by being converted. Then we must let the characteristics of the sons of Issachar dawn in our hearts—making us willing to set ourselves aside, and die, so that Jesus alone may be exalted as King on earth. The more we do this, the more times of refreshing we will experience in God. As Peter prophesied, "And [God] shall send Jesus Christ, which before was preached unto you: Whom the heaven must receive until the times of restitution of all things, which God hath spoken by the mouth of all his holy prophets since the world [or the age] began" (Acts 3:20–21, KJV).

What will God restore in the time of restitution? Scripture says that "Eye hath not seen, nor ear heard, neither have entered into the heart of man" all that God will do (1 Corinthians 2:9, KJV). Paul also says:

And do this, knowing the time, that now it is high time to awake out of sleep; for now our salvation is nearer than when we first believed. The night is far spent, the day is at hand. Therefore let us cast off the works of darkness, and let us put on the armor of light—ROMANS 13:11.

It's time for the restoration of all things. Those who have the desire to see the kingdom of Christ restored to Him know this, because they are being prepared in their hearts. They are not getting caught up in the temporal events of the world. They refuse to submit themselves to the lust of the flesh, the deceitfulness of riches, or the pride of life. They don't care about positions on their job, or money that men can offer them. They sense that this is the time of the Lord. They are turning their hearts and lives over to God in humility so they can be in on this Last Day move of God.

My Prayer

My prayer in this hour is that God will give us the holy boldnes that came upon Paul, who surrendered himself to the service of God.

> Then Paul stood in the midst of the Aereopagus and said, "Men of Athens, I perceive that in all things you are very religious; for as I was passing through and con-

sidering the objects of your worship, I even found an altar with this inscription: TO THE UNKNOWN GOD. Therefore, the One whom you worship without knowing, Him I proclaim to you"—ACTS 17:22–23.

Paul told his unbelieving generation, "You don't know Him, but I do, and I'm going to declare Him to you!" And he went on to announce:

God, who made the world and everything in it, since He is Lord of heaven and earth, does not dwell in temples made with hands. Nor is He worshipped with men's hands, as though He needed anything, since He gives to all life, breath, and all things—ACTS 17:24–25.

With boldness we are to declare that God, who does not need anything from mankind because He has given us all life and breath—this God loves us and gave His life for us. We are to tell them,

[God] has made from one blood every nation of men to dwell on all the face of the earth, and has determined their preappointed times and the boundaries of their dwellings, so that they should seek the Lord, in the hope that they might grope for Him and find Him, though He is not far from each one of us—Acts 17:26–27.

The visitation is here! The Bible says *God is not far from us!* May God not let this generation pass without bringing His visitation to us. *Amen.*

endnotes

1 Andrew Murray, *Humility*. Gainesville, FL: Bridge Logos, 2000, p. 31.

2 Teresa of Ávila, quoted in *The Wisdom of the Saints*. Jill Haak Adels. ed. New York: Oxford Press, 1987, pp. 37–38.

3 Augustine of Hippo, *Expositions on the Psalms*. Citation for Psalm 120:6. Available online at *http://www.newadvent.org/fathers/1801120.htm*.

4 Brother Lawrence, *The Practice of the Presence of God*. Available online at *http://www.practicegodspresence.com/edition/presenceofgod.html#letters*.

5 C. H. Spurgeon, "Baptism—A Burial," Sermon No. 1627

(October 30th, 1881). Available online at *http://www.spurgeon. org/sermons/1627.htm*.

6 Spurgeon, "Salvation of the Lord," Sermon No. 131 (May 10, 1857). Available online at *http://www.spurgeon.org/sermons/ 0131.htm*.

7 "The Most Remarkable Woman of This Age." *Commonwealth*. July 17, 1863. Also appeared in *Freeman's Record*, March 1865. Available online at *http://vi.uh.edu/pages/mintz/ 35.htm*.

8 Walker, Walter. *Extraordinary Encounters with God*. Ann Arbor, Michigan: Servant Publications, 1997, pp. 92–93.

9 Wesley, John. *The Works of John Wesley*. Thomas Jackson, ed. (1872 edition). Available online at *http://gbgm-umc.org/ umhistory/wesley/charmeth.stm*.

10 Augustine, *Confessions*, translated by Albert C. Outler. Available online through the Christian Ethereal Library, *http://www.ccel.org/a/augustine/confessions/confessions-outler1.0.RTF*.

11 *Susanna Wesley, The Complete Writings*. Charles Wallace, Jr., ed. New York: Oxford University Press, 1997, p. 73.

12 Benjamin, Earl of Beaconsfield Disraeli, *Contarini Fleming*. Part iv. Chap. v. Quoted in John Bartlett, *Familiar Quotations*, 10th ed., 1919.

13 Catherine Marshall, *Meeting God at Every Turn*. Carmel, NY: Guideposts, 1980, p. 98. Quoted in Walter Walker, *Extraordinary Encounters with God*. Ann Arbor, Michigan: Servant Publications, 1997, p. 121.

14 Ibid., p. 122.

15 Ibid.

16 Ibid., p. 123.

17 Aleksander I. Solzhenitsyn, *The Oak and the Calf: Sketches of Literary Life in the Soviet Union.* New York: Harper & Row [1975] 1979, 1980, p.7.